Everything
You Want to Know
About TM—Including
How to Do It

Everything You Want to Know About TM—Including How to Do It

John White

PARAVIEW
Special Editions

New York

Everything You Want to Know About TM—Including How to Do It was originally published by Pocket Books in 1976.

Cover design by smythtype
ISBN: 1-931044-85-6

Library of Congress Catalog Number: 2004102009

CONTENTS

5

Everything
You Want to Know
About TM—Including
How to Do It

Chapter 1

THE TM PHENOMENON

In 1975 one of those legendary publishing events happened—the kind that every new author dreams about. The book *TM*: Discovering Inner Energy and Overcoming Stress* was published and rocketed to the top of best-seller lists around the country. Within six months of publication it was holding down the number two spot on *The New York Times* listing.

As I watched the action, I was both amazed and delighted. Only a few months earlier I had spoken to Michael Cain, one of the authors of the book and the man who had initiated me into TM (which is a registered trademark) in 1970 while he was teaching at Yale. Michael and I have become good friends over the years. He is a highly intelligent, dedicated, and humble person, and he has been very helpful to me in my work as a writer-editor and consciousness researcher. In 1972, when I was preparing my anthology *What Is Meditation?*, I asked Michael if he would contribute a chapter on TM. He graciously consented and told me that he was working on a book of his own with co-authors Dr. Harold Bloomfield, then in residence at Yale's Department of Psychiatry, and Dennis Jaffe, another meditator who was using TM to help rehabilitate drug addicts in a radical therapy project he was conducting in New

9

Haven. (Michael had conceived the book and had then asked Harold and Dennis to join him; however, it was ultimately agreed that Harold would get top billing on the cover since he had an M.D. degree.)

Michael offered to adapt sections of the book they were writing—the same one that eventually became *TM** (at the time they were calling it *Creative Intelligence Through Transcendental Meditation,* and later it was known as *Meditation and Stress* for a while)—for my anthology. Dennis Jaffe took on the yeoman's work of putting the chapter together, and it developed into the section called "What Is Transcendental Meditation?" in my book. I was extremely pleased with the piece because, like the others, it presented TM from the point of view of those well versed in that particular meditative tradition. You'll find the piece reprinted as an appendix to this book.

Michael called from the New York Academy for the Science of Creative Intelligence in Livingston Manor, New York, where he was taking advanced training in TM, about a month before *TM** was published. He wanted to know if I could suggest any people who might be helpful in publicizing the book. I was only too glad to cooperate, and gave him the names and addresses of some of the major book reviewers.

He described to me some of the publishing woes that had plagued him and his co-authors. The original publisher with whom they had contracted had broken the contract, thinking the book would be a loser. A second publisher, Delacorte, had bought it and had changed the title to *TM*,* but again delays had set in—the book had been scheduled for press, but the schedule had slipped and slipped again. Then Maharishi Mahesh Yogi —the founder of the TM movement, who had agreed to read and comment on their book—had been late in returning his approval. Discouraging events all, but the book finally made its way through production to finished copies—and a first printing of seventy-five hundred copies. That, Michael said somewhat sadly, was because

Delacorte didn't expect the book to go anywhere. Delacorte hoped they might sell out that small printing, but there were no plans to go into a second printing.

When *TM** took off in the Los Angeles area, where SIMS—Students' International Meditation Society, one of the American organizations that carries on the TM movement—has its headquarters, Dennis Jaffe reported by phone that booksellers couldn't get copies in stock for a while because of Delacorte's dim view of the future of *TM**. As I said, it was a rare publishing event.

In 1975, the year the TM movement refers to as "The Year of Fulfillment," another book about transcendental meditation captured the number one spot on the paperback best-seller lists. *The TM Book,* a cartoon-filled collection of short questions and answers and illustrative charts, is about as different in format from the scholarly *TM** as you can get. But it, too, zoomed up the best-seller lists. And then another legend was born. Warner Paperback Library bought the rack-size paperback rights to it for $550,000!

On the day in September 1975 that I heard about *The TM Book* being sold to Warner, I received one of the regularly issued newsletters from SIMS telling about the phenomenal growth of TM. The opening paragraphs read:

Maharishi Mahesh Yogi inaugurated the Transcendental Meditation Movement more than seventeen years ago in Madras, India. The results that were realized by meditators in the Movement's early days provided a basis from which Maharishi could envision a fulfilled society. In 1958, Maharishi embarked upon the first of many tours with the purpose of making the TM technique available by establishing "centers" throughout the world. In order to achieve this, Maharishi personally trained several thousand teachers of the TM program.

By the mid-sixties, interest in the Transcendental Meditation program took firm hold in the student

world and chapters of the Students' International
Meditation Society (SIMS) were established on
most U.S. campuses. Today, more than a decade
later, SIMS continues to flourish.

In March 1970, the first scientific paper that documents the benefits of the TM technique in objective,
verifiable terms was published in *Science* magazine.
This scientific data, along with the continuing favorable reports by meditators of improved mental and
physical health, stimulated interest in the TM program by people from all segments of society. The
early seventies was a time when thousands began
the TM program each month, and the conception
of a World Plan center for every one million people
was fully implemented to make the TM program
easily available to everyone throughout the world.

The year 1975 has witnessed the greatest growth
in the history of the Movement. The TM program
and the Science of Creative Intelligence (SCI) have
captured the attention of the world, and individuals
are beginning Transcendental Meditation in unprec-
edented numbers. This great increase in the number
of meditators in the world, with their increasingly
profound effect on society, has encouraged Maharishi to declare "the Dawn of the Age of Enlightenment." With the enthusiasm and assistance of meditators, the Movement will continue its rapid growth.

The newsletter continued with a few columns specify-
ing just how well the movement was doing in terms
of gaining new members. Under the heading "Vital
Statistics," the following appeared:

Presently, there are 580,000 meditators in the
United States and well over one million meditators
in the world. During the first six months of 1975—
"The Year of Fulfillment"—the following numbers
of people were personally instructed in the TM
techniques in each of the four U. S. regions:

East Coast—43,532
Western U.S.—26,040
Midwest—22,556
South-Southwest—15,630

A total of 107,758 people were instructed in the TM technique during the first half of this year.

The page ended with the traditional TM closing used on literature and letters—"Jai Guru Dev," meaning "Praise Guru Dev." Guru Dev taught Maharishi both the technique and the philosophy that have resulted in the current phenomenon called transcendental meditation, which has every indication of continuing its remarkable expansion and growth.

The vast majority of people in western societies are woefully ignorant about consciousness alteration and spiritual growth. (These are the key elements offered by TM, though they are usually packaged in more appealing terms.) It is essential that an attempt be made to peel away some of the layers of mystery surrounding TM and to explain as clearly as possible exactly what TM is, exactly how TM is done, and exactly where TM fits in with the whole realm of consciousness alteration and spiritual growth.

As I glanced through the SIMS newsletter, I thought of my own part in that phenomenon. If it's nothing especially significant, at least I've had a good look "inside TM"—a good enough look that I feel qualified to write this book. My purpose, plain and simple, is to offer a perspective from which TM can be evaluated, *outside* the ideological framework that so far has directed every book about TM and nearly all the other published literature on it.

Although I don't consider myself to be an *experienced* meditator—TM or otherwise—I have been deliberately engaged in the exploration of consciousness for some years. I have also been fortunate enough to associate with many people who *are* very experienced in meditating. Therefore, I'm taking the position here—perhaps presumptuously, but I hope not immodestly—of being knowledgeable enough that I can look at TM with a professional eye, so to speak, and offer some useful comments to the oftentimes naïve public who are being exposed to the TM message.

In this attempt to explore TM and to put it in some perspective, I'll share with you some of the experiences and insights I've gained regarding both TM and other meditative traditions and spiritual pursuits. I'll raise a note of caution and inject a word of skepticism where the idealism and enthusiasm of the teachers and/or practitioners of transcendental meditation seem to outweigh realistic expectations—but I'll try to do it fairly, with balance and good will. Throughout the book I'll try to call a fact a fact, an opinion an opinion, a speculation a speculation, and a rumor a rumor. (These are sometimes confused within the TM movement.) I have also included a brief glossary of terms and some suggested readings in the back for your convenience and further reference.

When I've finished, I trust it will be clear that, although I have some serious criticisms to report, this book is not an attack on TM, not a denouncement of Maharishi, not a "TM exposé." Some people have called the TM movement a scandalous ripoff bilking the public, and we'll look more closely at the spectrum of criticism surrounding TM later on. We'll also look beyond the TM mystique at the sometimes unbounded claims made by enthusiastic meditators who are themselves just barely in spiritual kindergarten. And after we've examined the evidence and the hearsay, pro and con, I sincerely hope that the uninitiated will be a little better informed and a little better able to decide whether or not TM is for them. I hope, too, that those within the TM movement will have their practice strengthened by new knowledge and a broadened perspective.

Maharishi has written, "One word from a man reveals his inner quality. . . . The extent of a man's evolution can be judged by a single word uttered by him." I'm uttering a lot more than a single word here. But if I were to utter a single word, it would be "love." Honesty is based upon love of truth. Helpfulness is based upon love of people. My wish here is to be honest and helpful. If this book helps some, wonderful! If it disillusions others, so be it. And if it angers still others, I can only say, I may disagree, but I don't mean to be disagreeable. What follows is offered in the spirit of love.

Let's begin.

Chapter 2

THE TM TRIP

Transcendental meditation is defined by SIMS as "a simple, natural, and effortless mental technique, practiced twenty minutes twice a day. During meditation, the individual experiences progressively quieter levels of thought until he transcends thought and experiences its source—the field of pure creative intelligence, that silent, unbounded state of awareness that gives rise to all impulses of thought, feeling, and action."

Maharishi says in his book *The Science of Being and the Art of Living* (published in paperback as *Transcendental Mediation*) that TM brings the attention "to the level of transcendental Being." It is a system, he says, of "turning the attention toward the subtle levels of thought until the mind transcends the experience of the subtlest state of thought at the source of thought." This process of refining the nervous system and expanding consciousness involves selecting a "suitable thought"—called a mantra—and then "experiencing it in its initial stages of development." Thus the conscious mind can "arrive systematically at the source of thought, the field of Being" from which all of creation springs.

In the course of a meditator's progress toward the source of thought, according to Maharishi, he passes through different levels or states of consciousness. There are seven states of consciousness in Maharishi's map of

17

reality, and only when you get to the seventh can you know reality fully. We all experience the first three—sleeping, dreaming, and normal waking. But when we begin the practice of TM, Maharishi says, we begin to transcend these three states. Transcend means to go beyond. Therefore, he calls the fourth state—which is experienced immediately in TM—transcendental consciousness. Beyond it are still greater states of awareness —cosmic consciousness; god consciousness; and the highest condition that the human mind and nervous system can reach, unity. (Anthony Campbell, an English medical doctor and a teacher of TM, has written an excellent book, *Seven States of Consciousness,* that provides a detailed description of each of these states.)

TM, or a technique similar to it, Maharishi insists, was the means that led to the insights on which all the great religions of the past were founded. In the course of time, however, this knowledge was lost and religion degenerated into form without content. Maharishi's work, which he first named a "spiritual regeneration movement," is to revive this lost knowledge, although he maintains that TM is not a religion.

My interest in TM began in about 1967, when I was doing graduate work at Yale. TM had made inroads there and was becoming an established part of the scene among both students and faculty, although on a very modest scale. I noticed posters about the movement here and there; I heard talk about it now and then. Its heavy claims were being registered in my data bank as something to consider as I proceeded in my self-study program of consciousness research.

By 1970 the reports reaching me were of sufficient strength to make me activate the data bank and see how it computed. It "computed" favorably, so I decided to take the TM course. Unlike most people who get into TM, however, I wasn't searching for myself or for happiness and inner peace. I had already received those gifts in abundant measure, thanks to a delivery some years earlier from the Cosmic Blessings Service. My experience with TM began as a deliberate exploration rather than as the sometimes desperate search that attracts many people to TM.

By starting with no expectations, just a desire to see what TM was all about, I had nothing to lose or gain. I feel I was able to "check it out" with less bias (which was, if anything, favorable) and a more comprehensive view than those who have a psychological investment in it.

Michael Cain initiated me on a beautiful autumn afternoon while his wife Charlotte and another initiator supervised several others who were also beginning the TM trip. I had brought the items required for the initiation ceremony—a clean handkerchief, some sweet fruit, and some flowers. Michael performed the ritual, sang the Sanskrit song in praise of Guru Dev and earlier teachers, and then passed my mantra to me. That's the term that's used —passing the mantra. Michael did it by speaking the mantra aloud to me while gesturing with his hand for me to "come here" or follow him. I got the idea and spoke my mantra aloud: *"Sham."* I guess that's how you'd spell it in English—the *a* has the sound of "ah" and the word rhymes with "mom." (Don't try to use this mantra yourself later on when I give you instructions for meditating, because it's mine—bought and paid for!)

Michael listened to my pronunciation, correcting me by saying it over and over and having me imitate him. When my pronunciation was right, he began to speak it more quietly while gesturing with his hand for me to lower my voice too. I followed suit and soon I was repeating "sham" inaudibly. Then, at his command, I closed my eyes and continued repeating it silently in my mind. I was meditating!

He let me sit there for a few minutes, then asked me some questions to verify that I was meditating properly, and finally sent me to another room, where I meditated for a full twenty minutes. And that's how I began TM.

What did I experience? For one thing, just as SIMS claims, I found that meditating seemed to give me a strong energy boost during the day. And like nearly all beginning meditators, I had some "unusual" experiences. Once I fell asleep. Once I got so far into it that my head dropped to my chest, apparently cutting off my breath. However it happened, I actually stopped breathing, and I was startled out of my meditation by an involuntary gasp for air.

One meditation was memorable for its especially vivid effects. I went into a space where lovely, soft colors began to flow past me as if I were rushing through a tunnel with lighted walls. If you've seen the movie *2001: A Space Odyssey,* you'll know something of what I experienced. Recall that long psychedelic scene where astronaut Bowman is passing through the atmosphere of Jupiter, preparing to land. Brilliant colors seem to stream off the screen, rushing at the audience and disappearing behind them as the spaceship-theater drops through the Stargate. That's somewhat like my experience in meditation that particular day, except that the colors were unearthly, outside the visual spectrum.

Cosmic light shows are lots of fun, but they can be mystifying—and even addicting. I've met people who experience them once and think they're enlightened. If you're such a person, I hope you'll keep on reading.

What I liked best of all about TM was the delightful way that solutions to problems seemed to make themselves known. I don't mean problems in a psychotherapeutic sense. It's been my experience that there are no problems—for anyone!—there are only attitudes. And depending upon your attitude, a difficult situation can be regarded as a "problem" or as an exciting challenge and an opportunity to grow.

No, I'm talking about workaday situations at the office or around the house that had a degree of complexity, if not perplexity, so that an answer wasn't readily apparent. Meditation seemed to take care of them. The solution just came into my awareness fully developed, often with the script written out, so to speak.

And if the problem were of an intellectual nature—I enjoy that sort of headwork—meditating seemed to grease

the wheels there too. The problems would present themselves during meditation and then solve themselves. Ra-
tional analysis and logic weren't eliminated from the
picture either, because, as I considered the solution after
I was done meditating, it would appear altogether logical
and well thought out. Meditating, it seemed, allowed
certain processes to be speeded up enormously so that
the answer "popped in" as if it were a fully formed, direct
insight into the situation. This didn't happen every time,
of course, nor did just one meditation take care of a
particular problem every time. But the experience was
significant enough for me to want to report it here.

I followed TM procedure faithfully for six months and
then decided to "drop out"—I felt I'd learned enough
about it to satisfy my curiosity. I intended to get back
into a meditating routine at some later time, and in fact
I did. But while I wasn't meditating, I learned something
about the TM trip that isn't part of the course. I learned
that there are influences, both within yourself and from
others, that tend to pressure strayed sheep back into the
fold.

When I mentioned to some meditators that I'd stopped
TM, a subtle change came over them. Some were genuinely concerned for my well-being and gave me friendly
counsel, as if I had a psychological problem that required
attention. Their attitude was all right by me—I took no
offense. But someone less sure of himself than I was
might have started meditating again immediately out of
a sense of insecurity, just to feel the friendly, secure vibes
of group acceptance again.

To other meditators I was now an outsider, an alien,
no longer a true believer. Spiritual pride is the name of
that game. In Zen it's called Zen sickness. The basic
element—as always—is ego. It works like this: Just as
the ego is being subjected to a spiritual discipline designed
to reduce its deadly control on your life, it moves uplevel
on the whole scene and asserts a more subtle, more
sophisticated control by using the spiritual practice to
feed its incessant demands for status, for impressing

others, for making yourself look good by making others look bad. In various ways the people with ego problems let me know where it was at. "Gee, you're not meditating anymore. How awful! Well, I guess that shows who's got it together around here." Score one for the e-g-o team.

By no means was that typical of my relations with TM people, and it certainly isn't their prerogative alone. Spiritual pride takes a multitude of forms. Once I encountered it in a young woman—call her Sandy—who was a student in the classes of a well-known San Francisco guru. When I mentioned that I'd edited a book about higher consciousness, she immediately cut in to ask if I knew her teacher. At the time I didn't. Now I do, and I genuinely like and respect him. But all I could say then was, no, I didn't. "Oh, you ought to," Sandy said. "He's *so* high!"

Now, maybe he is—I tend to agree—but that's not the point. The point is that Sandy was using her studies and her friendly close relation with the guru to grab a little status. By basking in his glory, she could play "one up" on everybody, her ego told her.

And thus the game goes, with infinite variations—my guru is higher than your guru, my meditation technique is better than yours is, we've got more followers on our trip than you do, I can meditate longer than you can, my spirit guide comes from a higher plane than yours does, and so on and so on.

I point this out for whatever it may be worth as you look more closely at TM or any other trip. Don't be surprised and don't be disillusioned by the politics of consciousness-raising. You'll find the same hustling, gossiping, infighting, commercialism, and all-too-familiar game-playing that you know from every other human institution. If someone tries to flash his intimate knowledge of Maharishi on you or to otherwise impress you, don't judge TM by it. You'll see this boasting everywhere you look on the spiritual scene. Why? Simply because we're all human beings. As St. Augustine said, you should hate the sin but love the sinner. And remember that the work is always greater than the man—including the head man.

By and large, I found my TM experience to be enjoyable, refreshing, even exciting at times as various facts and previously compartmentalized areas of my knowledge seemed to grow together with experience.

But I never did experience what TM makes one of its major selling points—bliss. According to Maharishi, "Expansion of happiness is the purpose of creation." This statement appears in *The Science of Being and the Art of Living,* and it certainly tells you where he's coming from. No puritanical hellfire and damnation, no psychoanalytic guilt, no existential *angst* and absurdity. Maharishi shows in his own person something of what the expansion of happiness is all about. He laughs and giggles frequently; he apparently has a jolly time at whatever he's doing.

Unfortunately for Americans, they've been sold a bill of goods called "bliss," and at the level of mass communications, the TM people are tainting their own message by using that word. J. D. Salinger made a useful distinction in one of his stories—joy, he said, is a liquid, but happiness is a solid. Most people don't know that. They mistake momentary euphoria—bliss—for happiness. Joy, euphoria, rapture, bliss—they're evanescent, they don't last. Like liquids, the tighter you try to hold them in your hand, the faster they escape through your fingers. Happiness is of a different character. It's a more mature, enduring experience. It lasts and it doesn't depend on getting high. Bliss is a peak experience; happiness is a plateau experience.

Now, there's nothing wrong with bliss. You can get it from walking through a forest, watching kids play, even from reading a book. But don't mistake it for enlightenment, especially if someone tries to sell it to you. Some of the trips you'll find today in the spiritual supermarket are designed to give the newcomer a taste of bliss right away. Get 'em high with heavy-breathing exercises to hyperventilate the brain or with autosuggestion to put 'em in dreamland and you've got 'em hooked. If you're naïve about altered states of consciousness and how they can be manipulated to induce a high*—and about 90 per cent of the American public are—you're likely to become a "spiritual addict" on that trip. And it may take anywhere from a few months to a few years before you climb out of that bag and begin to look for more stabilizing experiences based on character growth and cultivation of the mind.

So watch out for that word "bliss." If someone just has to tell you about how they got blissed out, listen and learn. When bliss is the name of the game, the game falls into the same category as the instant remedies for headaches and overeating that Americans have been conditioned to grab automatically instead of responsibly maintaining their health in the first place.

I remember an occasion at the New Haven SIMS center when this point was vividly impressed on me. I had gone there for a "check"—that's a follow-up procedure after initiation. You meditate under the guidance of a person, a "checker," who is trained to be able to tell whether you're meditating properly. The checker was very busy on this occasion, so he took me into the checking room with another man—call him Joe.

We went through the checking procedure, which is really a ritualized repetition of certain questions that the checker asks about your meditative experiences—he keeps asking the same questions until you give him the correct response. The "correct" response is based upon certain subjective events, and it indicates that you're meditating according to the TM procedure. After the checker has spent three or four minutes with you and started you meditating properly if you weren't following procedure, he leaves you to meditate for the full twenty minutes required for beginners.

So Joe and I sat there meditating. That's when I had the *2001*-like light show I described earlier. It was interesting, even intriguing, and refreshing. But that's all—nc

---

* See *Altered States of Consciousness* and *The Book of Highs*
Their authors and publishers are given in the list of "Suggested
Readings" in the back of this book.

"bliss." And I realized that day that the most fundamental thing you can ever learn intellectually about meditation is that you must observe experiences in a detached way. Nonattachment is the key—the key to solving the "problems" of living. If meditation has any value whatsoever in helping people to get their acts together—and that's the primary claim of TM—it resides in teaching them to experience life with detachment. And detachment means *not striving* to get something or somewhere, regardless of whether your goal is a beautiful skyride, improved health, better grades, or enlightenment.

Detachment is not indifference, and detachment does not prevent intelligent action. Detachment means giving up desire, for desire is the mainstay of egotism. As the *Bhagavad Gita* says, "Perform every action with your heart fixed on God. Renounce attachments to the fruits. Be even-tempered in success and failure, for it is this evenness of temper which is meant by yoga"—yoga meaning "yoke" or "union" with divinity.

I chose that quotation for two reasons. First, the *Bhagavad Gita* is the most sacred book to Maharishi. Remember that he is a Hindu monk and that TM is rooted in yogic tradition. (Am I restating the obvious by pointing out that his last name is Yogi?) My second reason takes us back into the checking room.

Joe and I had finished meditating and the checker was now making himself available to answer any questions we might have about our meditation or about TM in general. I had none. But Joe—bless him for his honesty —asked a stunner. He sat there quietly, the way you usually do when you come out of meditation, explaining to the checker that he'd been meditating faithfully for the six months since he'd been initiated and had only missed one meditation the whole time. He was really dedicated about it, he said, and had noticed some changes in his life—he didn't get so angry at minor upsets and didn't argue so much with his wife anymore. Then he dropped a question into the quiet room that showed that he, too, had been sold that old bill of goods. "That stuff's okay," he said, "but where does the bliss come in?"

You see what I mean?

Let's be clear about this: TM is beginner's meditation —highly simplified mantra yoga packaged in a brilliant way. (How far you might go with it is one of the questions we'll deal with later.) There's no need for embarrassment at being a beginner—everyone is, in some way. But beginners are, by definition, ignorant and therefore open to error, false belief, manipulation by the misguided and unscrupulous, and so forth. To the extent that these elements are present within the TM movement, beginners can be hurt. As we go along, I'll try to point out where I think this is happening or might happen. For now, though, let's have a sort of introductory lecture for beginners so that you can see more clearly what meditation is and how TM fits into the big picture.

Chapter 3

WHAT IS MEDITATION?

One of the first things you must do in order to see TM in perspective is to learn that there are other meditative traditions. Maharishi acknowledges this, but he also says that TM is a more efficient technique for enlightenment than any other. You'll sometimes hear TM people use an analogy that started with Maharishi and which says that TM, compared to other techniques, is like a car compared to a horse and buggy. If you want to reach enlightenment the fastest way, take a car named TM.

Maybe so. For the moment, however, let's just take a bird's-eye view of meditation. Stand by to get high!

Meditation is a time-honored technique for helping people to release their potential for expanded consciousness and fuller living—in fact, it's probably humanity's oldest spiritual discipline. There will never be a better world until there are better people inhabiting it, and meditators claim that the best way for people to change is by "working on" themselves through meditation.

As a technique for assisting in the process of enlightenment and knowing self, ultimate reality, or God, some form of meditation appears in nearly every major religious and spiritual tradition. The entranced yogi in a lotus position, the Zen Buddhist sitting *zazen,* the Christian kneeling in adoration of Jesus, and the Sufi dervish

27

whirling in an ecstasy-inducing trance—all can be properly described as practicing meditation.

Whatever its form, the undeniable appeal of meditation lies in the fact that the core experience of meditation is an altered *state* of consciousness leading to altered *traits* of consciousness. In the altered state, your ordinary sense of self—your ego, your "I"—is diminished, while a larger, more fundamental sense of self-existence-merged-with-the-cosmos takes over. The diminishing of ego and self-centeredness carries over into normal waking consciousness, and from that changed way of relating to others and to the world, you begin to get all sorts of wonderful benefits on all levels—physical, psychological, social. General health and stamina improve. Tension, anxiety, and aggressiveness decrease. Personal and family relations also improve. Meditators say that meditation changes their lives.

In psychophysiological terms, meditation appears to induce a *fourth* major state of consciousness. It's not sleeping, dreaming, or normal wakefulness. Body functions usually slow to the condition reached in deep sleep, yet the meditator remains awake and emerges from meditation with a feeling of rest and relaxation. The table on the opposite page will give you an idea of the kinds of things that happen.

In the more advanced stages of meditation, mental and physical stillness is complete. The meditator is totally absorbed in a peaceful state having no particular object. His consciousness is without any thoughts or other content; he is simply *conscious of consciousness*. In yoga, this emptiness of consciousness without loss of consciousness is called "samadhi." In Zen, it is called "satori." In the west, it is best known as "enlightenment" or "cosmic consciousness" (although Maharishi uses the term "cosmic consciousness" to designate a level of consciousness well *below* the highest state of consciousness but above normal wakefulness).

This state of consciousness contains a paradox that is always experienced and reported by soul travelers to the highest regions of the spirit. The paradox is this: With

COMPARISON OF METHODS FOR INDUCING THE RELAXATION RESPONSE

(Reprinted by permission from "Your Innate Asset for Combating Stress" by Herbert Benson, M.D., in *Harvard Business Review*, July/August, 1974.)

Technique	Physiologic measurement					
	Oxygen consumption	Respiratory rate	Heart rate	Alpha waves	Blood pressure	Muscle tension
Transcendental meditation	Decreases	Decreases	Decreases	Increases	Decreases	Not measured
Zen and Yoga	Decreases	Decreases	Decreases	Increases	No change	Not measured
Autogenic training	Not measured	Decreases	Decreases	Increases	Inconclusive results	Decreases
Progressive relaxation	Not measured	Not measured	Not measured	Not measured	Inconclusive results	Decreases
Hypnosis with suggested deep relaxation	Decreases	Decreases	Decreases	Not measured	Inconclusive results	Not measured
Sentic cycles	Decreases	Decreases	Decreases	Not measured	Not measured	Not measured

the emptiness comes a fullness—unity with divinity, knowledge of humanity's true nature, and, to use a phrase from St. Paul, "the peace that passeth understanding."

I like the statement about meditation by Anagarika Govinda, a German who became a Tibetan Buddhist lama. Lama Govinda says that meditation is "the means to reconnect the individual with the whole—i.e., to make the individual conscious of his universal origin. This is the only positive way to overcome the ego-complex, the illusion of separateness, which no amount of preaching and moral exhortation will achieve." An awful lot to be expressed in so few words.

To attain the state of cosmically conscious selflessness —a state valued by all spiritual traditions above material wealth, fame, and status—many forms and techniques of meditation have been developed. Some are passive; the yogi sits crosslegged with so little motion that even his breathing is hard to detect. Other forms of meditation, such as tai ch'i, involve graceful body movements. Sometimes the eyes are open; sometimes they are closed. Sometimes sense organs other than the eyes are emphasized— beginners in Zen pay attention to their nasal breathing. In other traditions, sensory withdrawal is dominant and attention is drawn *away* from the physical senses. Some meditative techniques—TM is one—are silent; some are vocal with chanting. Some meditations are private; others, such as a Quaker meeting, are public.

You can see that a wide range of approaches exists. The silent forms of meditation center on three techniques —concentration, contemplation, and the mental repetition of a sound.

TM is just one of the forms of meditation that emphasizes the repetition of a sound, which may be a single syllable such as "Om" or a word, phrase, or verse from a holy text. Many Christians use the Lord's Prayer as the basis for meditation. A Zen technique involves use of a koan, an apparently insoluble riddle such as "What is the sound of one hand clapping?" that the meditator mentally examines.

In contemplative forms of meditation, the eyes are

open so that the meditator sees a yantra, a form on which he centers his attention. The focus of attention may be a religious object such as a crucifix, statue, or picture. It might also be an inscription, a candle flame, a flower. Or the meditator might use a mandala, a painting or drawing that, typically, has a square-in-a-circle design of many colors symbolizing the unity of microcosm and macrocosm. All objects of contemplation serve the same purpose.

Concentration is generally considered the most difficult form of meditation. In most concentration techniques, an image is visualized steadily in the mind. It could be the thousand-petal lotus of the Hindu and Buddhist traditions, or it could be the crescent moon of Islam. It could be Judaism's Star of David or the Christian mystic rose. Sometimes the mind may be held free of all imagery and "mental chatter"—this is a clearing away of all thought —or the attention may be focused at some part of the body. The mystical "third eye" located at a point midway between the eyebrows is often used in this technique; also common is the so-called "concentration on your navel." This phrase shows a misunderstanding of the process of directing your attention to the abdominal area about two inches below the navel and simply becoming one with your breathing, flowing into awareness of the rhythmical, cyclical body process by which life is sustained and united with the universe.

It should be clear that meditation cannot be defined in a sentence or two, although many have tried—some with excellent results. One of my favorites is from Krishnamurti's *Think on These Things:* "Meditation is the process of understanding your own mind. If you don't understand your own thinking, which is self-knowledge, whatever you think has very little meaning. Without the foundation of self-knowledge, thinking leads to mischief. Every thought has a significance; and if the mind is incapable of seeing the significance, not just of one or two thoughts, but of each thought as it arises, then merely to concentrate on a particular idea, image, or set of words—

which is generally called meditation—is a form of self-hypnosis."

Definitions help, but it is direct experience that really matters. Historically, the goal of meditation has been a transformation of the whole person. Research data dramatically validate many of the claims that meditators make (although some serious questions about the research itself have been raised lately—see Chapter 6). Traditionally, behavioral changes that come with meditation are reinforced through voluntary conformity with the meditative ethos and life-style, and this is still ignored by meditation research, including the research on TM.

To what extent are behavioral changes and altered traits of consciousness due to peer pressure, group conformity, and the sharing of group beliefs? The research thus far gives no sure answers. Throughout history, however, teachers of meditation and spiritual masters have emphasized "right living" to support one's meditation. By that they generally mean a healthy diet; an honest means of income; association with virtuous and sympathetic people; truthful speech; kindness and humility in relations with others; a social conscience; and forsaking of egotistical desire for power, fame, prestige, wealth, psychic powers, and so forth.

The San Francisco psychiatrist Arthur Deikman recently made an interesting observation. "Probably the importance of meditation lies in changing a person's orientation towards living, not in its ability to produce dramatic changes in states of consciousness," he said. "It's fairly easy for a normal person to have 'unnormal' experiences, but people meditating without the supporting philosophy are less likely to be involved long enough for some of the subtle changes to occur or to change their orientation from *doing* to allowing things to happen spontaneously."

Meditation doesn't require extreme asceticism and withdrawal from society; the aim of meditation is to bring the meditator more fully into the world, not to encourage retreat from it. A religious retreat may be appropriate for some in the course of their meditative training and discipline, and this is another honorable tradition—the way of the monk, the nun, and the religious hermit. But obviously it's not for everyone.

Here it's important to note that meditation doesn't require you to sacrifice or abandon your intellect. It's been said that the intellect is a good servant but a poor master. Our society has made intellect its master. Consequently people are enslaved, somewhat off-balance; they live only from the neck up, out of touch with their feelings. And they limit their intelligence by mistaking intellect for the full spectrum of mental potential to act creatively. In meditation, the intellect's limitations become apparent, while other (usually unsuspected) modes of problem-solving and insight emerge, along with an improved ability to focus on learning.

It's no accident that students frequently report improvement in their grades and their ability to study after beginning meditation. Enlightened sages have always been acknowledged for being brilliant, high-I.Q. people with finely honed intellectual powers who have enhanced their meditation "research" through scholarly studies that cultivate the mind. Their writings and speech display a solid knowledge of tradition, clear logic, and a keen ability to analyze, discriminate, and reply quickly with a well-suited response. They use their intellects intelligently.

The best that can happen through meditation is enlightenment. Spiritual masters of all ages have been unanimous in declaring that through meditation people can "cleanse the doors of perception" and purify consciousness so that they come to know their higher self, God. Through direct experience—not book learning or intellectual word play and conceptualization—people can reach a state of conscious union with ultimate reality and the divine dimensions of the universe. In that state, all the long-sought answers to life's basic questions are given, along with peace of mind and heart. (I don't mean answers in the sense of scientific data or scholarly information but, rather, that the purpose and meaning of existence become perfectly obvious.)

There are other paths to self-realization and God-knowledge, of course, but meditation is one path easily available to many, and that's the chief reason for the worldwide interest in and enduring value of meditation. It is a tool for learning spiritual psychology and a technique for expanding consciousness—safe, harmless in most circumstances,* easy to learn, beautifully portable, available in endless supply, and legal!

The highest development in meditation, regardless of the "school" or "path," brings technique and daily life together. When learning and living are integrated in spontaneous practice, the meditator becomes what the Tibetan Buddhist teacher Chogyam Trungpa calls "meditation in action." Meditation is no longer just a tool or device, no longer just a "visit" to the fourth major state of consciousness. All four states are integrated in a manner of living that is best described simply as the *fifth* major state of consciousness. The meditator has so completely mastered the lessons of meditation that his entire life is a demonstration of the higher consciousness that can be experienced if it is sincerely sought.

People who have achieved this fifth state of consciousness have been recognized through the ages as special persons for whom attention and reverence are proper. (This doesn't mean they should be worshipped, however!) In them the alteration of consciousness called meditation has led to a *transformation* of consciousness. Changing consciousness changes thought; changing thought changes behavior; and changing behavior changes society. Thus the changed ones live as examples to others who are on their way to transformation of self and world.

This is the fullest development of every form of meditation. By changing yourself, you help to change the

---

* Borderline psychotics can bring on full-blown psychosis through meditation, although skilled teachers of meditation can guide them safely through to health if they are given time and suitable situations. In others, meditation can release suppressed memories and feelings that may make the meditator uncomfortable and uptight as he gets on with the process of unclouding his consciousness.

world. Personal evolution becomes social revolution—peaceful, powerful, permanent.

Now let's look specifically at the TM system of meditation.

Chapter 4

MANTRAS—THE SECRET OF TM

Mantras have traditionally been described as a tool for thinking—that is, for mind control or self-control of the mind. *Man* is a Sanskrit word meaning "mind" and *tra* means "control." Strictly speaking, the word *mantra* is plural, the singular being *mantram*. TM, however, uses mantra as singular—an understandable anglicization of the word.

Munishri Chitrabhanu, the New York-based spiritual head of some five million Jains throughout the world, recently described mantras this way:

Mantra are words that are used so that the meanings and positive vibrations can act as brakes on our minds, purify our minds, remove the roots of fear and negative influences. When mantra are chanted aloud or silently, they clear the vibrations in our minds and surrounding us, they help us to end our inward mental chatter, and they lift us to a higher level of consciousness. They are used to spread a feeling of universal consciousness.

According to Maharishi, a mantra is a sound whose effects are known. In TM, the sound doesn't have any intrinsic meaning as a word or syllable; in some other meditative traditions, the mantras do have meaning. In

TM the mantras are simply sounds in and of themselves, but they are *not* meaningless sounds that just pop into the head of the teacher or the meditator. The sounds are said to be special ones with vibratory characteristics especially well suited to the meditator's personality and mental qualities, and can therefore only be given by someone who has been taught the special science of sound by Maharishi during a teacher training course.

This may seem silly at first. It may even seem like a ripoff—"Step right up, folks. Get yer mantra here. Only a hundred twenty-five bucks! Hurry, hurry, hurry!"

But before you dismiss mantras as nonsense (which in a sense they *are*, since they don't have linguistic meaning), think about a little story that comes from the life of Ramakrishna. This God-realized man lived in the last century and is considered by many to be one of India's greatest saints. You can read about him and his teachings in a very fine book called *Ramakrishna: Prophet of New India*, written by his disciple, Swami Nikhilananda.

One day Ramakrishna was at the home of a friend, doing what he liked to do best—speaking about God. Among the group listening to Ramakrishna was a highly educated man who considered himself quite an intellectual. As he listened to the skinny little unschooled man who couldn't even read, his ego swelled. He felt that his modern education had "liberated" him from the ancient religious traditions of India that fettered people with dogma and ritual. To show his sophistication, he began to converse with Ramakrishna in a way that would, he felt, demonstrate his own learning and the saint's ignorance.

When Ramakrishna began to talk about meditating on the name of God or on one of the many names God has in Indian culture—in other words, doing mantra meditation—the man in the audience began to argue with Ramakrishna. He pulled all sorts of verbal tricks with logic and reason. He'd show up this benighted fool and the ridiculousness of using a mantra!

Ramakrishna held his tongue for a while; and then, at

a pause in the man's harangue, he said loudly, "Shut up, you idiot!"

This unseemly remark totally stunned the pseudo-intellectual because it was so out of keeping with what he had expected from the quiet, gentle saint. The man was shocked speechless. Then he started breathing hard and sat down, fuming and raging silently because he had been so humiliated in front of all the people he'd been trying to impress.

Ramakrishna let the man simmer for a little while as he continued addressing the group. Then he turned back to the man and said, "Please forgive me, sir. I didn't mean that to be taken personally, but rather as a lesson for everyone here. Just consider your condition right now. Your heart is beating rapidly. Your blood is racing through your veins. You're angry, you're breathing hard—and all because of one little word. Think about that, and then consider what might happen if you repeat the name of God to yourself regularly."

Words and sounds *do* have power—power to affect us deeply, power beyond their linguistic value. A terrifying scream in the night may have no verbal or cognitive meaning, but the chilling effect it can have is familiar. It is a powerful consciousness-altering device.

Maharishi is not the only one who claims to be an initiate into the ancient knowledge of the way in which sounds and vibrations can act upon human consciousness. It is considered to be a primary esoteric science by many other teachers of meditation both in and outside the yogic tradition. Maharishi himself says that he is only transmitting and reviving lost knowledge from a centuries-old oral tradition that was passed on to him by his own guru.

An example of such knowledge is the sound generally spelled "om" in English but pronounced "aum" in Sanskrit. It is supposed to be an approximation of the sound perceived by enlightened seers in a state of higher awareness as they penetrate to the mystery of creation itself and "hear" the material universe constantly coming into being. Thus, "om" is held to be a powerful mantra because of its cosmic-divine qualities—but I have heard from a checker that Maharishi doesn't recommend the use of it because, he says, it tends to make the meditator withdrawn.

There are many examples of the power of mantras. One comes from the biography of Swami Satchidananda, the head of the Integral Yoga movement who is presently living in America. His book, *Integral Yoga Hatha,* is one of the finest illustrated texts for self-instruction in yoga.

According to the biography, a young man came to Satchidananda to inquire about meditation and yoga instruction. He was chronically sick and coughed a lot. As the man was departing, Satchidananda asked him to wait a minute. Then he got a glass of ordinary tap water and blessed it by holding it in his hand while quietly chanting a special mantra over it. Apparently the mantra allowed Satchidananda to energize the water in the same way some psychic healers have done in laboratory tests by the laying on of hands. The man drank the water and then headed for home on the subway. Within twenty minutes he felt a powerful urge to vomit and bolted off the subway at the next stop. After vomiting a horrible black liquid, the man later reported to Satchidananda, he felt perfectly fine and the chronic condition never returned.

Satchidananda is a disciple of the highly revered Swami Sivananda of Rishikesh, India, who was responsible for instructing Satchidananda in the use of mantras. Another disciple of Sivananda's is Swami Radha of the Yasodhara Ashram in Kootenay Bay, British Columbia. Radha is one of the most fully realized beings I've met. She told me that she, too, had gotten some very dramatic effects from using mantras learned under Sivananda's guidance.

Let's accept the claim that TM mantras are based on an ancient tradition that is quite exact in its knowledge about the qualities and effects of sound on human consciousness. Does modern psychology have anything to contribute to our understanding of this matter?

Harvard psychologist Dr. Gary Schwartz made some interesting comments on TM in the April 1974 issue of

Psychology Today. In his article, "TM Relaxes Some People and Makes Them Feel Better," he said that one of the keys to the mantra is that it has "signal value." Because it is chosen for each student, who in turn must never disclose it, the mantra "becomes special for the student and therefore more likely to hold his attention and be used. It signals the meditator that he is about to feel deeply relaxed."

Dr. Schwartz also pointed out that the euphonics—the pleasant, soothing sounds—of the mantra are probably also important. "Psychophysiological research indicates that sounds that rise slowly and are resonant can decrease heart rate, inducing relaxation." He concluded that the mantra can help a person relax for physical reasons, as well as for reasons of expectation and suggestibility.

TM claims that the mantra it gives you is uniquely suited to the characteristics of your personality. Maharishi writes in *The Science of Being and the Art of Living:*

> Because each personality has its own quality, it is extremely important for each man that a special quality of thought be selected whose physical influence will be beneficial and useful to himself and to the whole world. The influence of a spoken word carried by waves of vibration in the atmosphere does not depend upon the meaning of the word. It lies in the quality of the vibrations set forth. Where it is necessary to produce vibrations of good quality for an influence of harmony and happiness, it is also necessary for the quality of vibration to correspond to that of the individual.
>
> Individuals differ in the quality of the vibrations that constitute their individual personalities. That is why the right selection of a thought for a particular individual is of vital importance for the practice of transcendental meditation.

But is it possible for TM to present this vast body of knowledge to students in training to become teachers within the short three-month period a course takes?* My opinion is that it is not.

I'm not a teacher of TM, nor have I taken teacher training, but I've spoken about this with other people. One man told me that he'd had to drop out of teacher training because of the need for a surgical operation. There were only three weeks left to his training, but the class still hadn't reached the point where they were to be trained in selecting mantras for TM initiates.

I've asked teachers of TM about the mantra training, but they're all pledged to secrecy, so I don't have the inside story on mantras from the TM point of view. But my reason and my experience tell me that three weeks of training or less can hardly do anything more than cover the subject in a hasty, "once over lightly," rudimentary fashion and give a few useful guidelines to be applied in rote, mechanical fashion. It simply doesn't seem possible for teacher trainees to master, say, the equivalent of a college freshman survey course in that short a period of time, let alone to receive the "advanced degree" that might be expected of an expert in mantras.

Moreover, most teachers of TM are relatively young and inexperienced people—some are only in their teens—whose knowledge of human psychology must necessarily be more textbookish than pragmatic. That's not meant as a putdown—it's just an observation about the inherent limitations of being youthful. You only have to practice TM regularly for two years before you're eligible for teacher training. And work history, educational experience, and other such criteria don't bar you if they're less

---

* Recently the three-month teacher training course was lengthened to six months. The schedule of events in the three-month course was so crowded and hectic that the training was anything but relaxing for some, and there seemed to be need for more training in teacher skills, so the training was broken into two three-month segments, Phase I and Phase II. Most of the old curriculum was moved into Phase II, while Phase I was given over to matters such as checking and lecture training. Substantive knowledge about TM is still pretty much reserved for Phase II, and a person is qualified as a TM teacher only after completing both phases.

than average for middle-class America. In short, just about anybody can become a teacher of TM.

I find it difficult to believe that in three weeks or less an inexperienced person can suddenly be turned into a sophisticated psychologist whose mastery of the occult knowledge of sound allows him to instantly assess another's personality traits with enough precision to choose a mantra suitable for him or her alone. It seems more likely that Maharishi has a small repertoire of mantras and some general guidelines for their use that he teaches to students.

I can't prove that—it's a calculated guess—but it coincides with what a checker who holds a Ph.D. in linguistics once told me. He hadn't taken teacher training, but he had spent several weeks with Maharishi in Colorado and was an insider of sorts. According to him, all of the mantras are recorded in Sanskrit texts written by ancient yogis but still available today, and what Maharishi has done is to choose some simple mantras from this selection.

That TM teachers themselves don't get any significant training at all in the background that produced the rules for formulating and selecting mantras seems a likely possibility, but the only way the public will ever know for sure is for someone on the inside to "leak" the information.

Some people have skeptically accused Maharishi of worse than just having a small bag of tricks that he recycles. The vow of secrecy about your mantra, they say, is to ensure that you won't tell yours to another meditator and find out that he has the same one, which is also the same one that the next guy has, and so on down the line.

I'd like to put *that* rumor to rest now. I know a meditator who persuaded two others to reveal their mantras to him. Since both were identical to his, it looked pretty suspicious until he persuaded a third meditator to open up. His mantra was different. And, to close the argument in favor of TM, I'll add that my own mantra is also different from the first two.

Another anecdote is pertinent here. In 1972, I attended

a planning meeting at the Institute of Living in Hartford, Connecticut. The Institute, prestigious in mental health circles, is a large, well-staffed private sanitarium—the oldest in America—with extensive facilities. Its director of research, Dr. Bernard Glueck, had become interested in TM's therapeutic effects because his son had begun meditating and had eventually become a teacher of TM. Both Glueck and his son were at the meeting, as were other research doctors and TM teachers. Also present were Gay Luce, author of *Sleep and Dreams* and *Body Time,* and Eric Peper, a biofeedback researcher.

The purpose of the meeting was to explore possible designs for an experiment that was later conducted there. This experiment would measure the efficacy of TM vs. biofeedback training of alpha brain-wave production as aids to therapy. (TM apparently proved more effective, and therapy combined with either TM or biofeedback training gave better results than therapy conducted without either. However, the research is now disputed, and we'll look at the controversy in Chapter 6.)

At one point the question of comparing mantras was raised, and one of the TM teachers responded as follows. When he was just beginning TM, he said, he got curious about the validity of his mantra. He wanted to test whether it was just something his initiator had pulled out of the air. So, unknown to the first, he went to another initiator. He was initiated all over again, and—lo and behold—the second initiator gave him the same mantra. Still skeptical, but less so, he went to a third initiator—and again he was given the same "personal" mantra suited to his particular mental traits.

Such an experience could be interpreted to mean that TM has just one mantra that every initiator gives to everyone he initiates. But as I mentioned earlier, an acquaintance of mine learned that that's not the case, and the meditator at the Institute of Living meeting was convinced by his experience not that it *was* the case, but that it could not *possibly* be the case. In fact, his experience convinced him to "stay aboard" and eventually become a TM teacher himself. So to those who question TM on the grounds of secrecy about mantras, my inclination is to say (in keeping with the TM tradition)—relax. I don't think you're being sold a bill of goods in that respect. You may be in others, and we'll look at those matters one by one, including the matter of *selling* anything at all. For the moment, though, let's get some personal experience with mantra meditation.

Chapter 5

HOW TO DO TM

I said earlier that there is no substitute for direct experience, and that's what I'll try to provide for you here. The following instructions are based entirely on my TM experience. There's no Zen thrown in, no meditation on light or color such as you get in Tibetan Buddhism, no concentration on the sound of your own heartbeat, no contemplation of a mandala.

But I must emphasize that this is a *simulated* TM experience—not the real thing. You're trying Brand X, so to speak, because theoretically TM can only be learned from a trained teacher of TM, which I'm not. The instruction includes several preliminary lectures and an initiation ceremony, plus some follow-up group discussions. TM teachers say that the teaching process is a very sensitive thing, that a lot of subtle factors are involved, that you can never get a true idea of TM from reading a book. That's why the tradition is an oral one; the need for an instructor, the TM people say, is fundamental. Maharishi would probably consider me to be violating the integrity of his mission by doing this. If so, I accept the blame—which is just what one TM teacher laid on me when I presented this "simulated TM experience" to an audience to whom I was lecturing on meditation. My reply to such people is that knowledge of what TM entails—how TM works—can be useful to outsiders when they try to decide whether TM may have value for them.

I think that's sufficient warning on the label for you. But before I get started I want to add two general remarks about when *not* to meditate.

Don't meditate after a meal. You can try if you like— it won't kill you—but most likely you'll only fall asleep. Your body has mobilized itself to digest food, and that means it's sending a lot of blood to the abdominal area. Blood flow through the brain is reduced so less oxygen is passing through the brain, and you get that sleepy feeling. That's why, unless you wait an hour or two after a meal, you'll probably end up dozing off when you try to meditate.

And don't try to meditate just before going to sleep— unless you want to stay awake half the night. After meditating, most people find themselves wide awake and bursting with energy, but meditation can't be regarded as a replacement for sleep. If you miss half a night's sleep because you meditate at bedtime, you'll be feeling it the next day.

Now, to do this simulated TM meditation, sit down on a chair or couch. Sit up straight but not rigid. Yogis say that your spine is your lifeline, and in meditation you should keep the central energy channel in your body—the spinal cord—free of any twists or curves caused by poor posture as you sit. In TM you may find that you relax so much that you sort of fall over to one side, or your head may nod down to your chest. That's okay, but if you become aware of something like that happening while you meditate, you should gently bring yourself back to the upright position.

Your hands can be folded or resting in your lap— whatever feels comfortable to you. If some part of your clothing feels tight or binding, loosen it so that blood circulation and breathing are unrestricted. Breathe through your nose unless there is compelling reason not to. Nasal breathing is preferable to mouth breathing in nearly all circumstances in life, and especially during meditation. Most people keep their feet flat on the floor when doing TM meditation, but you can sit crosslegged on a rug, yogi-style, if you want.

You can meditate in just about any environment, inside or outside. I was initiated into TM in a small apartment in New Haven, and noisy cars were driving by and kids were playing in the alley outside, screaming and shouting. If you decide to take up TM seriously, you'll get used to tuning out noises. But for this "test run" it would be best to choose a place indoors where the light is not too bright and the noise level is low. Make sure you're not going to be interrupted—take the phone off the hook and send the kids (if you have any) out to play with instructions not to disturb you for half an hour.

TM prescribes that you meditate for about twenty minutes each time. Since meditation tends to take you away from a timekeeping frame of mind, you should have a watch or clock arranged in such a way that you can easily see it without having to change your position. Then you can open your eyes slightly to see how long it's been. Don't be surprised if you think it's only been three or four minutes and then open your eyes to find that it's been fifteen. Meditation works that way. (With just a little practice, you'll develop a pretty good sense of when to come out of your meditation, and the watch or clock won't be necessary any longer.)

Now for the mantra. One of the Hindu names of God is Ram, pronounced to rhyme with "bomb." Ram or Rama—they're interchangeable—was the hero of the Hindu epic *Ramayana*. We'll use the name Ram in this meditation. The Hare Krishna people use it for chanting: "Hare Krishna, hare Rama." If you'd been raised in India, the name would have great significance for you, and if you've seen the film *Nine Hours to Rama* you know that it was the last word Gandhi uttered when he was assassinated. But since the name is essentially unknown to western culture, it will serve as a nonmeaningful sound for our simulated TM meditation. (Incidentally, the name Ram has been mentioned favorably for this purpose by two well-known gurus on the contemporary spiritual scene, Harvard psychologist-turned-yogi Ram Dass and the Indian psychic-spiritual leader Swami Muktananda.)

To begin, settle yourself comfortably into the meditating position that suits you. Sit quietly with your eyes open for a few moments, without any thoughts, and then close your eyes. For perhaps a minute just sit quietly without attempting to say the mantra. Most people normally breathe at a rate of about sixteen breaths per minute, so use your breathing as a guide for timing yourself. Just sit there and count sixteen breaths while you let your mind and nervous system cool down.

Then silently say to yourself, "Ram." You can say it at whatever speed you want, and you probably will find that you experiment a bit. Try coordinating it with your breathing, and say "Ram" as you breathe out. Just keep saying "Ram" silently in your mind over and over.

If your attention wanders away from saying your mantra—which it's almost certain to do unless you have truly extraordinary mental control—that's okay. That's part of the meditation process, according to TM. But as soon as you become aware that you have stopped saying your mantra, you should gently and effortlessly come back to it. Start repeating, "Ram, Ram, Ram."

During the time that your attention is off the mantra, all sorts of interesting thoughts and feelings and images may come into your mind. That's okay too. Don't try to stop them forcefully. Carefully but casually observe them, without becoming entangled in them or attached to them. You may start watching a lurid sex story or an adventuresome drama starring yourself, but when you become aware that you're not saying the mantra, gently let those thoughts go and begin to repeat the mantra again.

When you've decided to end your meditation, simply stop saying the mantra and sit there quietly for about two minutes with your eyes closed. Let your physical senses gradually restore themselves. Then slowly begin to open your eyes. Take the full two minutes to do so, counting breaths if necessary to time it. This is still part of the TM procedure, and it serves the vital purpose of avoiding shock to the nervous system, which is now in a very quiet and sensitized condition.

After the two minutes of "rising to the surface," your eyes will be fully open and you'll be completely aware of your environment. You may have moved your body, hands, or legs somewhat during your meditation—it's perfectly okay to do so—but you will probably now find yourself in a position that you've been holding in a relaxed way for five or ten minutes, maybe longer.

Stretch your arms, rub your face and eyes, and get yourself into motion. You'll feel like you're waking up after a good night's sleep, and maybe you'll yawn or heave a deep sigh. But within a few minutes you'll probably feel superawake and full of energy.

There you have it—a free lesson in TM. For those who want more, another free lesson can be found in the July/August 1974 issue of the *Harvard Business Review*. On page 49 of that issue you'll find an article entitled "Your Innate Asset for Combating Stress," by Herbert Benson, M.D. Dr. Benson is an associate professor on the staff of Harvard Medical School and was one of the early TM researchers. He first published his findings on TM meditators in *Scientific American* in February 1972. His co-author on that article was Dr. R. Keith Wallace, now president of Maharishi International University in Fairfield, Iowa. Dr. Benson is a man who knows TM.

What he did in the article for the *Harvard Business Review* was to adapt TM for use by the public at no charge, aiming especially for the uptight people who don't know how to let their natural physiological mechanism for relaxing do its work. Such people generally bring upon themselves a host of stress-induced ailments like high blood pressure (which could lead to heart attack), ulcers, and migraine headache.

In surveying various techniques for dealing with stress —including TM, Zen, yoga, autogenic training, progressive relaxation, and hypnosis with suggested deep relaxation—Dr. Benson found that they all had four common, basic elements for what he calls "elicitation of the relaxation response" (see chart on page 29)—in other words, how to relax. Those elements are a quiet environment, a mental device, a passive attitude, and a comfortable position.

Dr. Benson, who has written about this at length in his current bestseller, *Relaxation Response,* then devised "a simple, mental, noncultic technique" that he used with people acting as experimental subjects. The gist of the technique is this:

1. Choose a quiet, calm environment with as few distractions as possible.

2. Use the single-syllable word "one" as the "constant mental stimulus" (i.e., mantra) on which you focus.

3. Take a completely passive attitude—that is, avoid scrutinizing your performance critically or trying to force a relaxation response. Any distracting thoughts should simply be disregarded.

4. Sit comfortably. Loosen all tight-fitting clothing, remove your shoes if you wish, and support your arms and head.

Then, says Dr. Benson, proceed as follows, with your eyes closed:

> Deeply relax all your muscles, beginning at your feet and progressing up to your face—feet, calves, thighs, lower torso, chest, shoulders, neck, head. Allow them to remain deeply relaxed.
> Breathe through your nose. Become aware of your breathing. As you breathe out, say the word "one" silently to yourself. Thus: Breathe in . . . breathe out, with "one." In . . . out, with "one." . . .
> Continue this practice for twenty minutes. You may open your eyes to check the time, but do not

use an alarm. When you finish, sit quietly for several minutes, at first with your eyes closed and later with your eyes open.

The progressive relaxation of your muscles from toes to head is not part of TM—Dr. Benson added this procedure to the TM technique to help people relax more easily. But the rest is pure TM.

Dr. Benson's article is twelve pages long, and well worth reading for those who are trying to decide whether TM is for them. Part of it is reprinted as Appendix III in this book.

Chapter 6

THE SCIENTIFIC CASE
AGAINST TM

The claims that TM makes about its value for society are based on two sources of information. First, there are the subjective reports that meditators give about how their practice of TM has changed them. Second, and just as important, there is the research data obtained through objective scientific investigation. Let's look at the second source here, and at the subjective reports in the next chapter.

There is no small body of data on TM. Research into TM is an active field; as of July 1974, more than a hundred laboratories around the world—seventy in the United States alone—were investigating TM's psychophysiological effects. More than three hundred studies of TM have been conducted in twenty countries. SIMS Los Angeles keeps a current list (called the Scientists' Index) of active scientists doing TM research.

This research has tended to create a mystique about TM that few other spiritually oriented movements have. Science is the religion of our society and scientists are our high priests, even if they don't actively seek that role. If you can say, "Scientists have proven . . ." about something, an awfully big impact is made on most people. TM is capitalizing on that in a big way—sometimes legitimately, sometimes improperly—by publicizing TM research in a lavish, four-color P.R. campaign that must cost millions of dollars.

I'll assume you're familiar with at least some of the literature SIMS puts out on TM research and rather than discussing that we'll look at some TM research that isn't so favorable and that doesn't get included in the SIMS papermill.

At Stanford Research Institute (SRI), a giant brain factory in Menlo Park, California, more than three thousand people work on all sorts of scientific and social research projects for private industry, education, the government, and the military.

In 1973 Dr. Leon Otis, an SRI employee who had been initiated into TM, reported the results of a study he performed there "to determine whether unselected, non-predisposed subjects could learn TM and derive some of the benefits claimed for it by its adherents and proponents." Another purpose of the study was to test the reliability of earlier reports, which had claimed that significant physiological changes had taken place in subjects practicing TM, especially changes relating to psychosomatic problems. These claims were to be considered in terms of possible self-selection among TM meditators—that is, Dr. Otis wanted to see if the TM claims really *were* based on applying TM to the *general population,* or whether the people who came to TM and stayed with it were a specific type of person predisposed to get good results.

For a description of the manner in which Dr. Otis set up his research and compiled data, you can write to SRI for a copy of his report, "The Psychobiology of Meditation: Some Psychological Changes," which he presented at the American Psychological Association's 1973 meeting. The "meat" of his report follows.

First, Dr. Otis found that TM does *not* alter basic personality characteristics. From the results of the SRI experiment, he said:

> We might conclude that people who feel pretty good about themselves (or have few serious problems) tend to stay in TM, whereas those who [already]

feel [very] positive about themselves (or have more serious problems) tend to drop out. The degree to which people who stay in TM derive benefits from its practice appears to remain an open question. TM had no discernible effect in changing self-image over the year's test period for those people who continued in the SRI experiment.

Dr. Otis also found that claims of improvement in classical psychosomatic symptoms such as frequent headaches, insomnia, and fatigue were *not* time-dependent. A group that had been in TM only six months or less scored equal improvement with a group that had been practicing TM for more than eighteen months. According to Dr. Otis' interpretation, this fact indicated that "the influence of longevity in the practice of TM is questionable." He hypothesized that the decision to take up TM may be a crucial variable, and added:

As every knowledgeable clinician will attest, the decision to seek assistance and taking the steps to do so may be sufficiently "therapeutic" to the patient that he may terminate after only one interview, feeling completely cured and restored. This can be called a placebo effect, due to halo, or whatever. Yet it is well known that many such patients never again seek psychotherapy. Thus, for many people, the decision to take up TM and the experience of the instructional phase may be sufficient to result in an almost overnight change in at least *some* psychosomatic symptoms.

The report ended with a note about the possible dangers of TM. Dr. Otis suggested that TM is "a self-paced form of desensitization that also induces profound rest." "Desensitization" is the psychologist's term for letting repressed problems and feelings come into awareness. Dr. Otis noted that the beneficial aspects of rest are easily understood—a plus for TM. But, he continued, since desensitization may occur, "It would seem that those with insufficient controls to prevent the release of *massive uncontrollable anxiety* represent a potentially high-risk population for training in TM . . . without close supervision."

This warning was issued because some "casualties" had occurred during the SRI experiment. Two people in a control group using a simulated mantra that went "I am a witness only" dropped out of the experiment. So did three people in a group that was actually taught TM for the experiment. *All five* experienced the recurrence of serious psychosomatic symptoms that they had previously had under control. These symptoms included a bleeding ulcer that had been controlled for the previous five years; a repetition of depression requiring psychiatric care and medication; and extreme agitation that resulted in the loss of a job. "Although these events may have occurred for other reasons," Dr. Otis said, "their occurrence raises the possibility that TM may be counterindicated for some people—especially without close supervision."

Dr. Otis rewrote his report for publication in *Psychology Today* under the title "If Well-Integrated but Anxious, Try TM." (It was published in the April 1974 issue.) In less technical language, he wrote that TM works for some people, but that it is not a universal good trip. Although it can benefit a large number of people, he said, it was also his opinion that it will turn out to be "a waste of time" for many others. When TM works well, he said, it's working on *another type of person* from the one who finds it useless or detrimental. "This type of person is probably common in our society—someone reasonably well integrated, and yet bothered by neurotic anxieties, guilts, and phobias," he wrote. "Many such people are unwilling or unable to take their problems to a psychotherapist. They could benefit greatly from an easy form of desensitization such as TM."

Dr. Otis has been critical of SIMS. In Boston at the 1972 Biofeedback Research Society convention, I heard him state that SIMS had misused some of his data in a booklet of charts showing the results of various TM research programs. (More than one million copies of the booklet were eventually distributed.) The chart based on Dr. Otis' data showed that the longer people meditate, the more likely they are to give up drugs. This is true. However, SIMS *didn't* report that Dr. Otis had found that the data on discontinuation of drug use came from a group of people predisposed to stop in the first place, and that the discontinuation occurs, if it occurs at all, *within the first three months of practicing TM.* And you must remember that one requirement for initiation into TM is abstention from all nonprescription drugs for fifteen days.

Another critic of TM is Dr. Jonathan Smith of the psychology department at Roosevelt University in Chicago. For his doctoral dissertation, he conducted two experiments at Michigan State University to test the efficacy of TM in reducing anxiety and psychosomatic symptoms of anxiety. In personal correspondence he told me he "investigated only the psychotherapeutic potential of TM on highly anxious persons." He added that he did not consider himself a TM critic but a student of meditation who uses the scientific method.

Dr. Smith concluded that TM does indeed have psychotherapeutic potential. However—and this is the spark that may stir up a hornets' nest among TM researchers, as well as at SIMS—he told me that this potential appears to be due to factors *other* than the specific TM meditation exercise. "I propose," he wrote to me, that "the critical aspects may be (1) expectation of relief, and (2) a daily regimen of sitting with eyes closed."

Before looking more closely at Dr. Smith's findings, I want to point out that his statement correlates almost perfectly with one in Dr. Otis' report. At the end of three months, Dr. Otis interviewed the SRI meditators. The results suggested that "expectancy plays a critical role in whatever benefits accrue to an individual from practicing TM, and that an important contributor may also be the mere practice of sitting quietly in a relaxed posture."

In his as yet published dissertation, Dr. Smith notes that, since 1936, at least one hundred scholarly books

and articles have maintained that meditation is psychotherapeutic. Moreover, TM specifically has been promoted
as "a natural and effective cure for mental illness." The
purpose of Dr. Smith's study was to isolate the aspects
of TM responsible for its anxiety-reducing properties.

In his first experiment, forty-nine people were taught
TM by a local SIMS center and fifty-one were taught a
control treatment called Periodic Somatic Inactivity (PSI)
that Dr. Smith himself devised and named. PSI was designed "to match the content and form of all aspects of
TM indoctrination, including introductory lectures detail-
ing research and theory, formal instruction, and follow-
up meetings." (Particular care, he said, was taken to
match those aspects of TM that might foster expectation
of relief.) The PSI control treatment incorporated a daily
exercise similar to TM except that it involved "simply
sitting with eyes closed rather than sitting with eyes closed
and meditating." This experiment was a double-blind
study, meaning that neither the subjects participating in
the treatment nor the assistant teaching it knew that it
was in fact a control treatment.

The second experiment, using fifty-four people, involved a TM-like exercise and an "anti-meditation" exercise designed to be "the near antithesis of meditation."
The anti-meditation—which was a control treatment, not
a placebo—involved sitting with eyes closed and "actively
generating as many positive thoughts as possible." In
every other respect, Dr. Smith said, the two treatment
exercises were identical.

Both treatments were called Cortically Mediated Stabi-
lization (CMS), and were described to the people involved as an effective means of reducing anxiety. Neither
treatment was described as involving meditation. This was
done because Dr. Smith saw the impossibility of completely shielding people from seeing TM promotional
literature or stories about TM in the popular press. By
avoiding mention of meditation, he felt it would be less
likely that subjects would generalize the claims made
about TM to the treatments they were receiving in the
experiment. In addition, indoctrination was minimal for

both treatments; it consisted of an introductory lecture followed by three sessions of follow-up discussion and monthly "checking" sessions.

The final paragraphs of Dr. Smith's dissertation abstract are worth quoting:

> Results of Experiments I and II show six months of TM to be no more effective in reducing anxiety than six months of PSI and two and a half months of CMS Meditation no more effective than two and a half months of CMS Anti-Meditation. However, *all* treatments are significantly more effective in reducing anxiety than *no* treatment. These findings support the conclusion that the critical therapeutic agent in TM is something other than the TM meditation exercise.

But if the TM meditation exercise isn't responsible for TM's therapeutic effects, Dr. Smith asked—what is? He answered his question with these words:

> . . . One possibility is that sitting with eyes closed, regardless of whether or not one meditates, is therapeutic for some people. All four treatments studied in this project involved sitting with eyes closed on a regular basis, and all were found to be effective. In addition, a strong argument can be made that TM's therapeutic potential is largely due to expectation of relief. Both TM and PSI control treatments in Experiment I contained expectation-arousing factors previous studies have found to be highly potent in increasing or decreasing the effectiveness of a treatment. These factors are: (1) belief on the part of a treatment agent [subject] in his treatment's effectiveness, (2) credibility derived from the complexity and sophistication of treatment methods and materials, (3) accompanying claims and theoretical rationale, and (4) credible signs of improvement that the person receiving the treatment can observe for himself. The CMS treatments in Experiment II con-

tained these factors to *a much lesser extent*. And the TM and PSI control treatments were found to be significantly more effective than the CMS treatments.

Dr. Smith's assessment of TM and TM research doesn't end here. Like any good experimental scientist, he had reviewed existing literature on meditation research, including non-TM research, before beginning his first experiment. (Scientists do this to avoid "inventing the wheel" all over again.) Most of the literature dealt with TM. He reported his findings in the *Psychological Bulletin* (vol. 82, no. 4, 1975) in an article entitled "Meditation as Psychotherapy: A Review of the Literature."

One group of TM studies that he feels are virtually meaningless was done by mailing out questionnaires. The studies consistently yielded results favorable to meditation. However, Dr. Smith notes:

The major weakness of these studies is that they relied on data resembling solicited testimonials. A meditator asked to participate in a study investigating the beneficial effects of meditation might view this as an opportunity to "step forth for meditation" somewhat analogous to the evangelist's call to "step forth for Jesus." In both cases we are left wondering about those who remained seated. Put technically, the sample of those who volunteered to participate in meditation research was perhaps *not* representative of the population of those who learned to meditate. We cannot conclude from such studies that the practice of [transcendental] meditation is therapeutic.

Nor is it sufficient simply to test a sample of meditators before learning meditation and then after practicing meditation for some time. Dr. Smith found six studies of TM using such a design, and he discredits all of them. "Studies that compare changes experienced by meditators and non-meditators are faulted because the two populations may not be comparable." At the very least, he noted, meditators—by their very decision to learn meditation—show some motivation for self-improvement not demonstrated by nonmeditators. "Such motivated subjects may be ripe for growth and may display reductions in pathology regardless of what they choose to do."

Two further points in Dr. Smith's *Psychological Bulletin* article are important in his assessment of TM. First, he pointed out that there is a lot of research indicating that the expectation of relief "can render potent even the lowliest of sugar pills, and its absence can render impotent treatments that are ordinarily respected and accepted." Second, this expectation is aroused (if not deliberately) in people entering TM by the "believing, practicing meditators" who teach it and also by the two mandatory lectures preceding initiation that present "a plausible psychophysiological theory of the technique's effectiveness as well as summaries of numerous 'verifying' scientific studies."

The two other critics of TM I want to mention here take us right back to SRI, where they are employed. Dr. Demetri Kanellakos is an electrical engineer in the Radio Physics Laboratory and Dr. Jerome Lukas is a senior research psychologist. I've never met Dr. Lukas, but Demetri is a good friend who's been most helpful to me over the years by sharing meditation research data. He's also a dedicated teacher of TM who has spent much time with Maharishi, so if he has something unfavorable to report about TM, you can be sure it's not because he's biased against TM.

In 1973 SRI funded Demetri and Dr. Lukas to survey the research literature on TM. Their fifty-page report was later expanded into a book, *The Psychobiology of Transcendental Meditation,* which comprehensively reviews the published and unpublished scientific and popular literature (including books, articles, and newspaper stories) on meditation research—especially research on TM—available up to 1974. It's valuable reading for people interested in a deeper look at TM research.

Chapter 4 of their book is entitled "Are There Any Deleterious Effects of TM Practice?" The first point they note is one that Maharishi himself makes—namely, that stopping TM may introduce some "roughness" into the life of the person who has previously practiced it regularly. By "roughness," the authors say, Maharishi apparently means something akin to jet lag or the feeling you get when you have to change your sleeping habits. This roughness seems to be due to the meditator's becoming accustomed to new physiological rhythms—new body time—through the regular practice of TM. Later, however, they point out that Dr. Otis' study found that a meditator may at any time choose to discontinue the practice of TM without any apparent (long-lasting) ill effects.

The second point of their Chapter 4 concerns "unstressing." This is Maharishi's term, and it means releasing stress from the nervous system—stored stress that, through repression, has created "knots" or blocks that keep the nervous system from operating maximally. According to Maharishi, unstressing "balances" or "normalizes" the nervous system. Therefore, unstressing is ultimately a health-producing process.

Kanellakos and Lukas report that release of stress "may have some transient unpleasant consequences" but that these are almost always mild. They note that these stresses are hypothetical, not yet experimentally proven.

Meditators typically report that the normalizing phenomena of TM are of short duration, usually only a few seconds, and only after the fact does one realize that a certain symptom—due presumably to some deep-seated, unconscious stress—has disappeared or has been reduced in severity. At certain other times, however, when a "large block" of stress is being "dissolved," the unstressing phenomena may last a few minutes. If such a stress release takes place at the end of the meditation period and the meditation period is ended abruptly, psychological distress may be experienced for up to several hours afterwards. If such occurrences persist, it is suggested that the meditator consult his teacher, who has been trained to cope with such problems.

The authors point out that when you've ended a meditation period, "feelings of relief and satisfaction are typical, and these tend to reduce the negative effects felt during the normalizing process of meditation, whenever it occurs."

So it seems that TM can at the very least have some unpleasant effects that don't receive mention in the SIMS general literature. Granted that unstressing is usually only a minor discomfort of short duration, it can also be a lot more. One TM teacher told me of an unstressing experience he had about a year after being initiated. Halfway through a morning meditation he sensed a rapidly increasing feeling of heat that caused him to sweat profusely. Then a feeling of nausea took over and he had to vomit. Further meditation was out of the question because for the next two hours he had to huddle in bed, alternately perspiring and feeling chilly. While such unpleasant experiences are far from typical, you should nevertheless be aware that they may occur. Therapy isn't always pleasant.

And if, as Doctors Otis and Smith suggest, TM is effective in relieving psychosomatic disorders because you just sit and relax, there seem to be a lot of scientists doing very poor research—research with results favorable to TM that is being hyped by SIMS. I'm certainly not accusing anyone of deliberately trying to deceive the public. But as I've said, a note of caution and skepticism seems necessary in view of the evidence that TM has positive results during the first few months because of meditator motivation and the placebo effect. I hope that future, well-designed experiments will settle the question of TM's efficacy as psychotherapy—and the question of exactly why it works.

The need for some skepticism about TM was vividly underscored by an article that appeared in the October 3, 1975 issue of *The Hartford Courant*. Reporter David Rhinelander's front-page story about the highly touted TM research at the Institute of Living in Hartford, Connecticut was entitled "Disagreement at Institute Ends TM Use as Treatment." It speaks for itself:

A conflict over the value of transcendental meditation (TM) in treating mental illness has developed at the Institute of Living.

As a result, the technique is no longer being taught to patients at the four-hundred-bed psychiatric hospital.

Institute researchers have studied TM for the last three years. Dr. Bernard C. Glueck, director of research, has concluded TM has helped more than half the two hundred eighty patients who have been trained to meditate with the technique of Maharishi Mahesh Yogi.

But Dr. John Donnelly, psychiatrist-in-chief, says, "Our findings did not indicate any significant difference in the treatment of psychiatric disorders."

Donnelly said Thursday that since TM depends on teaching its users a secret word or "mantra," it violates the ethics of medicine and cannot be tested scientifically. Without proof of its effectiveness, he said, it cannot be considered a treatment.

During the three-year project, the Institute paid to have TM teachers train patients. But Donnelly said it would be unethical to charge patients for an unproven technique now that the research aspect of the project has ended.

He also said Institute patients would not be allowed to learn TM at local training centers because it would interfere with their hospital treatment. . . .

Glueck says the shutdown of the TM program comes just as he is collecting data that proves its usefulness. The research psychiatrist spoke Thursday at the twenty-fourth annual scientific symposium of the Connecticut Academy of General Practice.

He told the meeting that TM had helped young patients remain drug-free after they had left the Institute and that it helped older patients with severe anxiety and moderate depression to recover.

TM was used in conjunction with traditional treatments at the hospital, Glueck said, and careful comparisons with non-TM patients showed meditation increased the expected success rate.

Brain-wave studies of the meditators showed TM increased the waves associated with calm well-being and decreased those that produced anxiety and tension.

Patient profile studies showed a decrease in depression, anxiety, and antisocial behavior among the successful meditators and that the repressed feelings that caused the mental illness were released.

Glueck said just how TM works scientifically is unclear. But, he added, the indications are that meditation helps the brain to function in harmony and slows disruptive brain waves.

TM is useful among the general population, he said, because it can decrease stress, halt a buildup of tension, and prevent mental illness.

But Donnelly said at the Institute that TM benefits are found in "those who believe in it."

He said because TM depends on repeating the magic "mantra" word, it cannot be subjected to controlled studies that would use nonsense words instead of the mantra phrase. . . .

Beyond the question of TM's usefulness in psychotherapy, I hope that science will turn to the matter of assessing the *long-term* effects of meditation, including TM. In other words, after you've "normalized" and shed your psychosomatic problems, where do you go from there? Why settle for being normal? If you're well, can you get "weller"?

Only the schools of humanistic and transpersonal psychology seem to be concerned with the question of growth beyond normality. They recognize, however, that the major spiritual traditions loudly answer "yes," you *can* get "weller," and regard meditation as a central technique in spiritual development toward enlightenment. For working on yourself, they say, meditation is the best thing in the spiritual tool kit.

True? Or are these millennia-old traditions only preserving ignorance and illusion? Science has barely begun to investigate the notion of higher consciousness, and we're a long way from widespread agreement about consciousness itself. In Chapter 9 we'll look at what may be an important early step in this area.

For now, it's important to note that TM research thus far tells us nothing about higher consciousness, despite all the P.R. that SIMS pumps out. The reason for this is simple—the public and the scientific community have not been told in clear, specific, and testable terms what characterizes "higher consciousness" at each stage of enlightenment. Therefore, scientists have not been able to identify subjects on the basis of such criteria, nor have they been able to design experiments to test various psychological effects, physiological correlates, etc. Learning how to relax isn't higher consciousness, nor is unstressing, nor is becoming more energetic. The scientific community needs to be given guidelines so that subjects who are clearly in the cosmic consciousness, god consciousness, or unity consciousness stages of enlightenment can be selected without having test results diluted by meditators who aren't in that state of consciousness. Until this is done, all the claims about TM and higher consciousness cannot be said to be supported by science.

Chapter 7

THE CRITICS OF TM

In the last chapter we looked at the evidence from science that tends to dilute the TM mystique. In this chapter we'll look at what kind of criticisms people in the humanities have to make of TM. Let's begin by scrutinizing the subjective claims that TM meditators make about how TM has affected various aspects of their daily lives.

You can read some of the first-person claims, if you wish, by asking for *TM, Some Results* at any SIMS center. This collection of testimonials covers just about every aspect of daily life. Among the innumerable benefits that accrue, according to TM meditators, are self-actualization, peace within oneself, increased energy levels, loss of anxiety, relief from psychosomatic symptoms, happiness, greater utilization of creative potential, better academic performance, a decrease in use of drugs (both prescription and illicit) and alcohol, better sleep at night, giving up smoking, increased learning ability—in short, fulfilled living.

These claims, if accepted at face value, would indicate that TM is indeed God's answer to the cultural forces threatening to take Planet Earth right down the tube. The only hitch is that just about every other movement concerned with raising consciousness has its share of people making the same claims. They can trot out testimonials—

some from well-known personalities—just like the ones the TM people like to lay before you.

When I was director of education at the Institute of Noetic Sciences, one of my responsibilities was to screen the stream of people who came in to talk with the founder and president, Apollo 14 astronaut Edgar Mitchell. They came in all manner of garb and gab—from yogis to straight business people, from psychics to psychotics, from high school kids to sweet old ladies in sneakers, from M.D.s to hippies. And they came from every shelf in the spiritual supermarket. There were disciples, practitioners, devotees, proponents, adherents, chelas, and followers of every possible prophet or movement—Guru Maharaj-ji, Sun Myung Moon, David Michael the Cosmic Messiah, Hare Krishna, Sai Baba, Swami Muktananda, Eckankar, Timothy Leary, Scientology, Ananda Marga, and at least two dozen others—including TM. And if they couldn't get there in person, they'd call or write long letters, attaching descriptive brochures about their particular trips.

Many of them were perfectly wonderful people—together, stable, aware—who simply wanted to say hi and share their being in a supportive way. But would you believe that *half* of them felt that they had a monopoly on truth? I'm exaggerating, of course, and it's unfair to judge an entire organization by just one person, or just a few. But after hearing the same song, second verse, six times a day, I started to think, "Lord, protect me from gurus!" Whether their thing was mediumship or macrobiotics, Space Brothers or carbogen therapy, the enthusiastic people who presented it invariably had The Answer. Yet their claims about the personal benefits of their particular path to self-realization seemed identical to what I've just cited about TM.

In no way should this be interpreted as a putdown of anyone. It's not. What I *do* intend is to indicate that there are stages of spiritual growth, and that most of the enthusiasts who trooped into the Institute of Noetic Sciences were making claims typical of a very early stage—what I call spiritual kindergarten.

As an example, let's think of a teenager who's just fallen in love. A few years ago, most likely, the kid would have nothing to do with kids of the opposite sex. Then there was some intermingling at, say, junior high school dances or parties—shy intermingling at first, and then more bold. This was followed, perhaps, by a lot of dates with a lot of people. And then—*wham!* The Right One happens and it's love, it's Romeo and Juliet, it's the greatest thing in the world, it's an experience (the lovers say) that no one else could possibly understand because there has never been a love like ours.

It's almost a cliché, of course, to repeat the story from this point on. The wild longing for each other that nobody in history could ever have known before is probably familiar to nearly everyone. But you can't tell that to the young lover. Instead, he's got to tell you and the whole world about this transformative experience he's had called "falling in love."

And so do the people who suddenly blossom with their first taste of heightened awareness. From the cosmic perspective, that's a beautiful thing—another sentient being has stepped up a rung on the ladder of consciousness. And nature has arranged it so that its beauty is magnified by sharing it with others.

But just as you can get tired of hearing the same love story from teenager after teenager, even though you respect each one, so too you can get tired of talking to people who are still in spiritual kindergarten. Their stories are all real and valid, but not one is the last chapter in the saga of the evolution of consciousness. Many more adventures await the individual on the path to enlightenment —not the least of which is getting over addiction to "peak experiences" or to the guru who first turned that person on. That doesn't mean that anything is wrong with peak experiences, incidentally—only with the desire for them, which comes from a nasty thing spelled e-g-o.

TM doesn't tell you about any of this. No one admits that the TM claims may apply with equal validity to many meditational systems and consciousness-expansion courses; they only say that the research hasn't been completed yet.

And you don't hear about "the dark night of the soul" that has universally awaited those rare human beings throughout history who have attained cosmic consciousness—the time of anguish and suffering *after* they have gone through the initial stages and "peak experiences" from which, as far as I can see, the TM claims originate.

Nor is TM candid about the matter of the beliefs that are part and parcel of TM. This may be because most TM teachers themselves are unaware (or only vaguely aware) of certain fundamental assumptions behind their teaching. Some of the ones I've met have been quite dogmatic, with a set rap that they learned in teacher training to which they doggedly adhere in debate. Thus you can hear them insisting, as I did on a radio show recently, that TM is *not* a religion and that it requires you to believe nothing.

In reality, however, the rich variety of Hindu and Vedantic tradition plays an important part in TM. Maharishi's entire cosmology, with its levels of consciousness and theistic summit, are part of a belief system that you must tentatively accept if you are to operate within the TM framework. Later your belief may possibly become direct knowledge through the self-validating experience of enlightenment—but *every* spiritual tradition works this way; you've got to believe first. I'm not saying there's anything wrong with it—only that TM isn't exactly upfront about it and that many of the TM teachers ignorantly parrot the "party line" without realizing that they're not telling the truth.

In fact, it was the Hindu theology that enabled some fundamentalist Christians in Sacramento, California to successfully block TM's becoming a required course in schools there in 1973. The TM initiation ceremony is conducted partly in Sanskrit—at one point the initiator chants a song in praise of Guru Dev and various Hindu deities. An English translation of the ceremony revealed to the fundamentalist group that the initiator was invoking "foreign" gods. On that basis, they declared that a required TM course would be forcing school children to learn a particular religion, thereby violating the principle of separation of church and state. SIMS had to do a quick about-face, and their new posture offers only lectures on the Science of Creative Intelligence (which we'll look at in the next chapter) during school hours, leaving actual instruction and initiation into TM as a voluntary "lab course" after school hours.

Other TM beliefs include these:

1. Each person has within himself a source of experience that, when contacted, is the source of certain healthful benefits.

2. The pursuit of pleasure and happiness is a valid and accepted human activity. TM is harmonious with this activity and may even facilitate it.

3. Worldly achievement ("success") is also a valid and accepted human activity, which is harmonious with and can be facilitated by TM.

4. Drugs are undesirable. Drug experiences are incompatible with meditative awareness.

Speaking for myself, I can accept all of these on the basis of personal experience and philosophic analysis, but others may not be able to. I don't want to get into an extended discussion of these points here—I simply offer them for your consideration. Now I'll turn to what some other people have to say about TM.

One of my good friends is Jerome Ellison, an author and educator who has spent many years in dedicated service to humanity. Recently his efforts have been directed to a new organization, The Phenix Club. Because Jerry went through TM teacher training about five years ago, he has incorporated meditation into the structure of The Phenix Club, which, in its totality, is a "free friendship association of men and women who seek to improve the quality of their lives by reading, discussion and contemplation." (Those interested in more information can write to The Phenix Club, Box 25, Guilford, Connecticut 06437.)

I mention the foregoing because Jerry, as an experienced TM meditator who's spent considerable time with Maharishi, has some strong but well-meaning criticism to offer about the TM movement. The Phenix Club directly incorporates his TM experience as part of its suggested program, and it attempts to face clearly those areas where it sees TM as being weak.

TM's rampant commercialism, Jerry says, has oversimplified the process by which people attain wisdom and spiritual maturity. He directly attributes this problem to Maharishi, whom he finds quite likeable but nevertheless a shrewd merchant and showman. "TM people say that TM is easy, requires no brains, and involves no suffering," he told me. "It claims to be the solution to all your problems and promises pie in the sky. This is a travesty on what spiritual growth really involves."

Maharishi has disguised suffering with the word "unstressing," but Jerry says that suffering is one of nature's foremost remedies for restricted consciousness. It is one of the signs we get to tell us that something is fundamentally wrong and needs changing. To masquerade it as "unstressing" in a message that says "You don't have to change your life-style" is to subvert nature and ignore dangerous symptoms.

Nor does TM deal with the question of values, especially the superficial values that permeate our society and have led so many people to so much suffering in pursuit of instant happiness, Jerry adds. Our fundamental need is for *wisdom,* which depends in great part on a close examination of our values. There is nothing in TM about this—nothing about building character. TM glosses over this and instead pushes "success" and "enjoyment." As the public interprets this it means, for example, that corporate executives can continue their mad scramble to the top of the heap while sleeping better at night, having relaxed consciences, being untroubled about ripping off the public, exploiting workers, and plundering the planet.

It also means that rampant conspicuous consumption—

only lately slowed down by unforeseen economic forces—can continue unchecked as we "enjoy" life more through material pleasures. No need to give up anything, especially the ego-rooted desires that lead to all this insanity!

And this misinterpretation means, to give another example, that military people don't need to change their life-styles either. Through TM they can more efficiently and "successfully" plan for war. They can increase their reflex time and serenity as they pull the trigger. No need to deal with the issues of militarism, nationalism, and international power struggles. No need to consider the morality of it all.

Another criticism of TM comes to me from a businessman who asked to remain anonymous. He also pointed to the areas of character growth and values as the two in which the TM movement is lacking. TM, he said, does nothing to encourage meditators to cultivate the moral virtues of honesty, compassion, courage, humility, patience, and so forth—the qualities traditionally associated with self-realized people. Because I feel his words are worth considering, I'm going to quote at length from a letter I received from this person. It refers to a TV show on which some enthusiastic people told about the ways in which TM had helped them to become more successful and happy.

> . . . Their success is not the issue, nor is their happiness. We know how shallow those things are as they speak of them. What *is* important to consider is that none of these enthusiasts were known for their compassion or their brilliance or their contributions to mankind. They were mostly entertainers and politicians, people in categories notorious for being able to sense what is fashionable or popular at the moment.
>
> TM no doubt does help overstressed people to calm down. But . . . in the animal kingdom, these kinds—the misfits—would be eliminated by natural selection. That's the way evolution works. Do you think nature is going to step aside and allow the

selfish, the money grubbers, the "entertainers," the political "wheeler-dealers" to rise to the top over the long evolutionary haul? Not on your life—for that would mean that in another twenty-five years those most able to cope with stress and continue to carry on doing the same old things, only "better," would grow in strength and power, and would create an even greater threat to life on the planet than we now have. *Yet that is exactly what TM implies.*

TM does not require one to live a spiritual life. One can be a dictator or a slave driver and still "benefit" from TM. But all great spiritual leaders have said that before one can hope to see God, one must become godlike. All genuine systems designed to lead to higher states of consciousness teach that one must lead a better life, attempt to become like a god. A god is an ideal personality, and in any language or any society, the idea cherished in the hearts of people is someone who is loving, compassionate, truthful, benevolent, wise. Benevolence would demand that if someone has something of real and lasting benefit for his fellow man, he would make it freely available and would never set a price on it.

Development of character is not a prerequisite with those in command of TM. TM merely relieves one of his conscience. But we should not want to soothe our consciences, especially at this critical juncture in our planetary life. We need to cultivate an even greater ability to perceive our character flaws, and we need to strive mightily to overcome them. The further well-being of the race demands it.

It was interesting to see these criticisms echoed in a cover story in the October 13, 1975 issue of *Time.* It quoted two of Maharishi's countrymen who feel that TM is simplistic, overstated, and a palliative for the moral sense. Dr. Kumar Pal, secretary of the Yoga Institute of Psychology and Physical Therapy in New Delhi, said, "It is merely a technique, a very limited technique, and it is not yogic because it lacks the prerequisites of yogic meditation. A moral life is the *sine qua non* of yoga practice. The students and admirers of Maharishi Mahesh Yogi have no need to give up sex, liquor, and other immoral habits. They are reveling in immoral habits at the cost of basic moral values."

The publisher and editor of *Spiritual India,* A. K. Krishna Nambiar, made this comment to *Time:* "TM can make you a better executive, but it cannot give you the spiritual ecstasy that other, more spiritual meditation techniques do. It can never lead the meditator to *turya,* the fourth and eventual stage of spiritual ecstasy that is the final aim of meditation. . . ."

The last criticism of TM that I have to offer here comes from the late Dr. Haridas Chaudhuri. Dr. Chaudhuri was a disciple of Sri Aurobindo Ghose, one of the foremost figures of the spiritual renaissance that began in India in the last century. After earning his doctorate in philosophy, Dr. Chaudhuri entered into the *ashram* life at Uaroville in Pondicherry, India; there Sri Aurobindo became his spiritual teacher. Years later, Dr. Chaudhuri came to America and established the California Institute of Asian Studies in San Francisco and the Cultural Integration Fellowship. He was a strong beacon for those seeking greater world unity, and Maharishi was among the spiritual figures whom Dr. Chaudhuri sponsored in promoting deeper cultural ties between east and west.

I asked Dr. Chaudhuri to write an original article for *What Is Meditation?* He contributed a marvelous piece entitled "Meditation: The Dangers and Rewards." Broadly speaking, he said, there are three kinds of meditation— conventional, unconventional, and creative. Although he didn't say explicitly in the article that TM was conventional meditation, he did make this clear to me in discussions and correspondence in which TM and Maharishi were subjects. Therefore I feel that some quotations from his essay are worthwhile.

The main technique of conventional meditation, Dr. Chaudhuri observed, "consists in shutting out from view disturbing ideas, thought vibrations and suggestions, and distracting emotional waves. The constant repetition of a mantra . . . is a powerful instrument for focusing attention upon one's article of faith [the guru and the system of concepts and values that he represents] or for building up a mental fortress against all intruding and alien forces, whether external noises or incompatible thoughts or distracting inner urges and impulses."

He noted that use of a mantra may be accompanied by use of a *yantra* or visual image (usually of the guru or a deity). "The mantra and the yantra together can successfully finish the job of desensitizing the mind to all alien thought systems and of transplanting the mind from one cultural system to another."

Dr. Chaudhuri then continued with these important words for those who seek true liberation and enlightenment:

> In other words, the traditional or conventional mode of meditation produces the condition of monoideism, to use an expression of William James, which serves as a safe anchor for the meditator. Lifted out of the tumult and turmoil of conflicting social forces, the meditator experiences profound peace and a wonderful feeling of liberation. He enters into the kingdom of heaven within the golden shell of his own psyche.
>
> But a heavy price is unknowingly paid for the transcendental bliss of conventional meditation. It involves the suppression of one's independent thinking, resulting in incapacitation for critical evaluation of the value system handed by the guru. No thought structure or value system can possibly express absolute truth, for the simple reason that it represents a certain degree of abstraction, as Korzybski would say, from the infinite fullness of concrete reality. Unthinking identification with a particular value system may produce a wonderful sense of bliss, and that is perhaps all some people are capable of attaining—at least in this life. But such an identification also closes one's mind to the vastness of the real and confines it within a conceptual prison house. It produces, no

doubt, some amount of liberation from worries and anxieties, but it also provides an escape from authentic freedom of thought and direct contact with the multidimensional Being. Providing an escape route from one kind of thought system from which the meditator felt alienated, it binds him hand and foot in another thought system—occult, supernaturalistic, metaphysical, or mystical. The latter may be more glamorous and exciting, but is nonetheless hypnotically binding.

If you have not read this chapter in the right spirit, you may feel that it is a blanket condemnation of TM and an evaluation of TM meditators as hopelessly superficial. I mean nothing of the sort. As I said, most of the TM people I've met seem to be decent, upright individuals genuinely searching for growth to higher being. But they rarely seem to have any clear sense of what that entails, and the TM message can lull the ignorant into a false sense of security. In Chapter 10 I'll try to look more closely at what "higher consciousness" and "enlightenment" mean. For now, however, I want to say plainly that the spiritual life cannot be defined in terms of psychophysiological correlates such as brain waves or the relief of psychosomatic symptoms or increased energy.

If you seek enlightenment you must be prepared for times of pain and suffering (that's a hard word, but there is no other) during which only steadfastness of purpose will carry you through—not to bliss, but to serenity. Nevertheless, history tells us that those who sincerely will themselves to know God won't be denied the experience —even if they don't meditate at all! Insofar as TM's message evades this and the clear examination of the issues of character growth and values, it is undermining its efficacy and misleading people. There are no shortcuts to self-realization.

Chapter 8

TM AND THE
MIND-BODY PROBLEM

The relationship between the mind and the body is a very old philosophical problem that has never been satisfactorily solved. Scientists haven't gotten much further than philosophers, either, so the subject is quite uncertain even in scientific terms. And even if we add up all the physiological and medical knowledge about how the *body* (including the brain and nervous system) operates, we have only the barest beginning of insight into what the *mind* is.

Some people feel that the whole "problem" is an illusion created by a trick of language, and that in reality there is no such thing as body distinct from mind. But this just isn't so. The evidence of psychic research shows beyond doubt that the mind can operate separately from the physical body. Telepathy, clairvoyance, precognition, and psychokinesis all give evidence of the mind's extending beyond the limits of the skin. And the considerable evidence from survival research, which is the part of psychic research that looks at the possibility of life after death, suggests strongly that mind can operate without a body at all.

Clearly, there is a mind-body interaction. On the one hand, various forms of matter can adversely affect our mental state—this is the case with drugs, water and air pollution, and food that is lacking in nutrients or is loaded with chemical additives. On the other, various mental problems are being eased and even eliminated by body therapies such as rolfing, polarity therapy, biofeedback, and the Feldenkrais and Alexander methods.

Psychosomatic medicine has shown how we can think ourselves into bad health and various dysfunctions; likewise, it has shown that we can restore bodily health through changed mental stances. One dramatic breakthrough has been the curing of cancer through specific imaging techniques employed by some meditations. (TM is *not* one of them.) Imagine curing yourself of cancer! That's just what you do—imagine, image, visualize. In other words, the body follows where consciousness leads. I tentatively propose this as the first principle of holistic medicine.

Yet there seem to be exceptions to the rule. How, for example, can we explain the fact that some of the most highly evolved people, such as the Indian saints Ramakrishna and Ramana Maharshi, succumbed to cancer? By all accounts they were experienced meditators with great peace of mind, unconcerned about their fate. Are there forms of cancer produced by inherent properties of the body that aren't amenable to control through mental techniques? Is there some other factor operative here? I don't know. I only raise the question about an aspect of the mind-body problem that I find puzzling.

The mind-body problem remains in an indeterminate condition, with intriguing insights—but no definitive answers—coming from all sides. Yet some of the claims that TM makes presume that the problem is solved. This naïve view can lead to vague and misleading—even false —statements and advertising.

An example of this came to my attention recently. A Florida newspaper printed an advertisement for TM that was supposed to convince people that they could tap their unused mental potential, and began with words to this effect: "Scientists know that people use only 15% of their brain capacity."

This is an impressive-sounding statement, but it's pure pseudo-science. In the first place, no scientist has ever measured 100 per cent of someone's brain capacity, so there is no way that "15%" could be determined. We've learned a lot about the machinery of the brain. We know, for example, that there are about ten billion neurons in the cerebral cortex (the "gray matter") through which electrochemical messages flash, and that in some fashion not yet understood, ten *trillion* bits of information are processed every second by this computer-like organ. But how these electrochemical impulses in the neural pathways become human experiences such as love, fear, trust, and creativity is a mystery.

In the second place, at the human level, mental capacity has almost nothing whatsoever to do with brain size. The largest human brain ever measured—two thousand cubic centimeters in volume—belonged to a very large-headed imbecile.

Finally, the generalization about "people" is false. Assuming that there could be some measurement made of what constitutes the full 100 per cent, the correct thing to say would be, *"On the average,* people use only 15 per cent of their brain capacity." You yourself might utilize much more than that, while the next person might utilize far less.

Let me give you an example of how uncertain our understanding about the relation between brain and "mind" is. A few years ago, alpha brain waves became a big craze. A lot of them supposedly indicated a state of deep rest, bliss, and many other nice things. Lots of people made lots of money by selling courses and machines that supposedly taught you how to turn on your alpha. Electronic yoga, they said—and people went wild over it.

But that bombed out, so the enlightenment marketeers had to escalate to theta waves, which had been observed by scientists to be present in Zen masters deep in meditation. Theta was the thing! Learn to turn it on and you've got enlightenment, creativity—the whole ball of wax.

Only it didn't work that way. I once asked Dr. Elmer Green, a pioneer biofeedback researcher who was among the first to investigate theta brain waves in relation to creativity, whether the production of theta seemed to be organically attached to any value system. In other words, if theta was all that high, we ought to see some clear indications in what people said and did that they were well along the enlightenment road because of their theta control, right? But Dr. Green put that sort of nonsense to rest with a very short remark. "Frankly," he said, "when my subjects are producing theta, I can't tell whether they're in samadhi or just getting creative ideas about how to rob a bank."

For all the glitter that was generated in the press about the magic of brain waves, it's now clear that when we measure cortical rhythms, we're making a very superficial observation—literally! Brain waves are measured on the surface of the scalp. While they may correlate with subjective reports about feeling nice or getting creative or being spiritual, the brain waves themselves are not the cause of those mental conditions. But it's precisely this notion that has led many people into various mind-development courses.

A TM teacher involved in setting up the biofeedback-TM experiment at the Institute of Living that I mentioned in Chapter 4 told me a very interesting story about brain waves and TM. One day he was asked to meditate while wired to an electroencephalograph. The scientists wanted to see whether he produced theta waves. So he began to work with his mantra, and after about five minutes, he told me, he was producing theta so abundantly and so strongly that he actually drove the EEG recording pen right off the graph paper. His theta production was beyond anything the scientists had expected—they were amazed. But what amazed *me* was his answer to my question about the *quality* of his meditation that time. You'd expect that he must have pierced the highest heaven and scored 100 on the enlightenment meter, right? Not at all. It was only a fair meditation, he said—nothing exceptional.

This indeterminate relation between physiological *measurements* and mental *experiences* has frustrated many materialistic scientists, who assume that mind and consciousness can be explained in terms of the properties of

brain matter and brain processes. You can read a lot
about split-brain studies and hemispheric dominance, and
it's true that such research gives us a greater understanding of the mind-body problem. But not enough, apparently, to satisfy one of the most eminent neurosurgeons
in the world, Dr. Wilder Penfield. In the Spring 1974
issue of *American Scholar,* he published an article drawn
from his recent book, *The Mystery of the Mind,* which
was published by Princeton University Press. In it, he
declared:

> . . . After years of striving to explain the mind on
> the basis of brain action alone, I have come to the
> conclusion that . . . it will always be quite impos-
> sible to explain the mind on the basis of neuronal
> action within the brain. . . . The mind is peculiar.
> It has energy. The form of that energy is different
> from that of neuronal potentials that travel the axone
> pathways.

In the next chapter we'll look at an intriguing and testable hypothesis that may be the key to the mind vs. brain
riddle that Dr. Penfield has, thus far, sought in vain—it's
the kundalini hypothesis. But what can we say *at this
point* about the mind-body problem?

Consciousness seems to be the key to it all. From the
"body" side of the question—physics and the neuro-
sciences—it has become clear that "objective" observations are not useful. The deeper we go in examining the
material world, the more obvious it becomes that "observation" is a process of interaction between energy fields
and that the interaction influences what was to have been
observed. The notion of the detached, uninvolved scientist
is a false one. The consciousness of the experimenter
turns out to be an unavoidable part of the experimental
solution.

And from the "mind" side of the question—psychology
and philosophy—analysis again reveals that consciousness
is the fundamental fact and that objectivity has been impossible all along.

A growing chorus of voices from all points on the circle of scientific knowledge is pointing toward the riddle of consciousness as central to scientific research. Yale physicist Henry Margenau writes in his introduction to Lawrence LeShan's *Toward a General Theory of the Paranormal:* "Consciousness . . . is the primary factor in all experience; hence, it needs and merits the fullest attention any science can bestow on it." Molecular biologist Gunther S. Stent at the University of California, Berkeley, notes in *The Coming of the Golden Age* that consciousness is *"the* central philosophic problem of life." (He also feels that it is insoluble by science.) Psychologist David McKay demolishes the mechanistic-materialist view that reduces consciousness to an "epiphenomenon" of the brain's electrochemical processes with these words: "My own consciousness is a primary datum, which it would be nonsense to doubt because it is the platform on which my doubting is built."

Underscoring this is the etymology of the word "consciousness." Formed by the union of two Latin words— *con,* meaning "with," and *scire,* "to know"—consciousness literally means "that with which we know." The scientific investigation of consciousness is burgeoning. I've listed some books in the "Suggested Reading" list in this book—those by Ornstein, Tart, Weil, and Musès and Young—that present the scientific approach to consciousness research. My own *Frontiers of Consciousness* may also be of use to those interested in this area.

What does Maharishi have to say about the mind-body problem? In *The Science of Being and the Art of Living,* he writes, "The individual mind is . . . a limited reflection of the unlimited cosmic mind or pure intelligence." Vedic philosophy maintains that consciousness (the universal field of creative intelligence, in Maharishi's terminology) divides itself into the mind that perceives and the organs of perception. Thus the body (of which the brain and sense organs are parts) is a gross manifestation of consciousness, while the mind is a subtler manifestation. When a person's state of consciousness changes, brain/body and mental functioning also change.

From the cosmic perspective, all is one. This is our true Self—the infinite, eternal creation sustained by the creator. But at lower levels (the relative rather than the absolute, Maharishi would say), consciousness assumes two forms—mind and matter. These two forms then interact to produce the human drama; they draw the veil of *maya,* illusion, across our awareness and produce the false self, ego, that hides our true Self.

Since reality is essentially spiritual in nature, the spirit can withdraw from matter and still retain the characteristic of intelligence (which is presumably what happens at death). Likewise, matter can operate within its sphere without "mentality" in the sense of waking awareness. This occurs every night when we go to sleep, and when patients in a vegetative state of coma are kept alive by machine after all brain function and vital signs are gone.

Mind qualities are modified by the matter qualities. Thus we have differing levels of intelligence, from genius to severely retarded, depending to some unknown degree on mind-matter interaction, and enlightenment, therefore, would seem to depend to some extent on physiological readiness. The practice of TM, Maharishi says, refines the nervous system by unstressing it so that the individual mind reflects more and more the cosmic mind.

Maharishi likes to quote a passage from the *Rig Veda* that is part of the wisdom literature in his tradition: "Knowledge is structured in consciousness." In other words, consciousness is primary, and the quality and accuracy of our knowledge are dependent upon the degree to which we purify or expand our consciousness. Muddled consciousness produces confusion, uncertainty, doubt— i.e., low-grade knowledge.

This position dovetails with that of the scientists quoted earlier. It follows, then, that for science to completely describe an event, it must also include a description of the consciousness that is observing the event. The same event will be seen or described or "known" quite differently by observers with consciousnesses of different qualities, and the purer the consciousness, the more clearly and fully the event is observed by the knower. (His own "interference" or "noise" is reduced.) That being so, objectivity in science has been impossible from the beginning, and true knowledge depends on the observer knowing him- or herself—self-knowledge is paramount. The observer must first observe himself—his real Self.

This is a fundamental premise on which TM—and every other meditative technique—is based. Through meditation, you can change your state of consciousness and thereby change your brain/body functioning and mental functioning. Through meditation, furthermore, you can expand your consciousness to directly experience the larger dimensions of the psyche that ultimately are cosmic in extent, and thereby gain absolute self-knowledge.

From the point of view of consciousness research, the scientific tradition and the spiritual tradition are essentially the same. Outwardly different in form, they are really both sides of the same coin—the coin called "the search for the truth about reality."

People have a stereotype of scientists as people who can throw a lot of technical data at you. But this isn't all there is to science. Remember that science comes from *scire,* and connotes *how* you know, not what you know. *Science is really a method of knowing rather than a body of knowledge.* Our accumulation of scientific data is endless, but as long as the scientific method is followed, the data should be valid. Scientific method requires that data be obtained by trained observers and be empirically verifiable. Research must then be presented to the scientific community for examination and validation. A clear description of the techniques and materials used is necessary in the presentation. After research is first presented, the procedures are carefully repeated by others. If the same results are obtained, the findings become accepted as scientific fact.

The essence of science is its method, not its data, and we have to recognize that the same thing is at the center of certain spiritual disciplines. Take yoga as our best example here, since it's the tradition from which Maharishi comes. When considered in the terms above, yoga can be called a science of consciousness—in fact, it is probably the oldest in the world. Why? Because it offers a method by which others can verify the information obtained by a previous researcher. As with official science, the steps to be followed (including postures, breath control techniques, meditation practices, dietary regulation, ethical restrictions, and rules for balanced living) are clearly delineated, and the "findings" (stages of enlightenment) have been uniformly reported in every century for thousands of years.

Spiritual disciplines can and should work hand in hand with science, for both seek to purify consciousness and improve the quality of knowing. Knowing is fundamental to knowledge, and the quality of any knowledge is dependent upon the quality of the knower.

The image of science and spirituality working hand in hand is a powerful one. As I have said, science is the religion of our society and scientists are the high priests. The aura of science is especially effective in selling something. Whether they're pushing better gas mileage or faster-acting headache remedies, the guys who put together the TV ads will want to feature some dude in a white smock with a "clinical report" in his hand telling you why his product is better than Brand X.

The TM movement recognizes this clearly and uses science to sell TM. The specific form it takes has a grandiose title—the Science of Creative Intelligence. SCI is one of the major selling points in the TM message, which, in its totality, claims to provide both the theory and practice of enlightenment.

The Science of Creative Intelligence is said to be the "first science" because it provides the unifying principle and fundamental basis of all knowledge—orderliness in nature. Since this is the basis that makes inquiry possible in any field of science, SCI integrates all fields in a natural, coherent way by laying out the concepts that uphold them. It takes into account the subjective aspect of existence as well as the objective, and thus it is holistic. A Maharishi International University pamphlet explains that "this science arose from the major discovery that there exists in every human being the constant source of intelligence, energy, and happiness." (Alert readers will recognize that phrase as a translation of the Sanskrit term *sat-chit-ananda,* one of the basic principles of Hindu philosophy.)

TM is the experiential or "laboratory" part of SCI that verifies the theory. "Through this simple and natural procedure alternated with activity," the same pamphlet states, "the whole mind and body gradually gain permanent access to the full value of creative intelligence." TM is supposed to allow you to systematically enjoy increasingly refined states of consciousness until you make direct contact with the field of pure creative intelligence. In this way, you can investigate the nature of the basic field from which all knowledge comes—that is, gain both *knowledge* and *experience* of the universal basis of existence.

TM and I are united in agreeing that the investigation of consciousness, experimentally and experientially, must be the central activity of science. Furthermore, my reason and my experience lead me to concur with the concept that consciousness—as the universal field from which all existence and knowledge come—is the unifying principle for science.

But there are some major contradictions and uncertainties that I personally would want resolved before I said I was fully satisfied with the presentation of SCI. First, how does the following statement by Maharishi, which comes from the *Proceedings* of the Inauguration of the Dawn of the Age of Enlightenment ceremony on January 12, 1975, square with what he and the TM publicity people have said previously? In the section dealing with SCI, Maharishi declares on page 41:

> . . . Consciousness is a holistic projection of the physiological activity in the brain. What consciousness is, is a holistic projection of the activity of all the neurons and all the cells—everything that the brain is composed of. That we know simply by our knowledge of different states of physiology with reference to different states of consciousness. . . . At

every change in the style of functioning of the physiology of the brain a different state of consciousness
comes along.

As I read that, it seems to be, quite frankly, a damning
statement. It contradicts both science and the Vedic tradition, not to mention Maharishi's own previous position,
by saying that consciousness is a result of brain matter and
brain processes. This is the ultimate materialist-reduction-
ist position, held by people such as Harvard psychologist
B. F. Skinner, the father of behaviorism.

According to this statement of Maharishi's, physiology
is the controlling factor in consciousness and awareness
is a secondary effect. If this is truly the case, the concept
of a universal field of consciousness is sheer nonsense.
Likewise, out the window goes the possibility of refining
one's state of awareness by directing it or letting it direct
itself. If physiology is almighty, how can one of its own
by-products ever control it?

Perhaps I'm not reading Maharishi rightly, however,
because in the same paragraph he says, "When a different
state of consciousness comes, a phase transition comes
with the change in the style of functioning of the nervous
system." *This* implies that consciousness is primary—an
analysis of this statement shows that consciousness comes
first and *then* the functioning of the nervous system is
modified (i.e., different brain waves are generated and
other physiological indicators change).

But unless Maharishi has given a new and peculiar
meaning to the word "consciousness," I don't see how
those two statements can be reconciled. They seem to
contradict each other and, as I noted, the first one contradicts the entire thrust of Maharishi's previous statements.

I also have questions about the concept of "unstressing" and "normalizing" the nervous system as the means
of refining consciousness. Dr. Penfield points out that
there seems to be an energy in the body—mind energy—
unknown to official science. Acupuncture theory holds this
idea quite specifically and calls the energy *ch'i*. It also

maintains that there are energy pathways in the body, called meridians, other than the nervous system. Science has partly demonstrated that meridians do exist through physiological experiments that have produced results inexplicable in terms of anything we know about nervous system functioning. Your mental state—from the point of view of acupuncture theory—may have little to do with the state of your nervous system, as long as those other energy pathways are functioning well and circulating the cosmic nonphysical energy, ch'i.

If this is so, there may be a major area of incompleteness—and possibly even basic error—in the SCI theory when it attempts to explain how TM works to refine consciousness. "Normalization" of the nervous system has yet to be demonstrated, and even if it does work to refine consciousness, unstressing may be only part of the real picture—how large a part, we can only guess at this point.

In yogic theory, *prana* is the counterpart term for ch'i. Prana is the nonphysical cosmic energy that underlies both mind and matter; it is the first form that consciousness takes as it manifests itself and brings the universe into being. Maharishi refers to prana in *The Science of Being and the Art of Living,* using the term properly in accordance with Vedic philosophy, so far as I can tell. In fact, he specifically says, "Prana is . . . the basic force of the mind."

Yet SCI and the TM movement never refer to the possibility of nonphysical energy, even though it is absolutely fundamental to the whole tradition Maharishi represents. After reading huge stacks of TM literature, including the inauguration proceedings, my feeling is that whatever science may be presented in support of TM and SCI, it is decidedly establishment, uncontroversial, and not in the same ballpark with that being practiced by scientists and researchers who are trying to pin down the nature of the psyche through the empirical method. How might the people putting forth the SCI position react, for example, to the possibility of a nonmaterial field of mind actually surrounding our planet like an atmosphere—an envelope of nonphysical energy outside the spectrum of forces presently recognized by science that enfolds and interpenetrates the earth and all its creatures, extending outward into space for an unknown distance?

Preposterous? Maybe, but it's in accord with Maharishi's tradition, and his own words imply it, although he himself doesn't state it explicitly, to my knowledge. But if he doesn't, others do, and it's my opinion that this concept is what will eventually resolve the mind-body problem.

We can compare the problem to broadcasting. The body is the receiving mechanism, with the nervous system (and possibly the meridians or some other system unknown to official science) acting the way the transistors, capacitors, circuits, etc. in a radio or TV set do. But the components alone, even in a fully assembled state of great sophistication, aren't sufficient for the operation called broadcasting. They must be energized—there must also be a carrier wave transmitted by a broadcasting station. In the case of a human "broadcast," the mind is the broadcasting station and carrier wave sending out its own program. Now, since a radio or TV set doesn't generate its own energy, it isn't logical to say that the brain/body generates *its* own vital force. Rather, it receives its energy from an outside source. What is that source? Consciousness. We can say, to complete the analogy, that consciousness is the designer of both the sending and receiving equipment, as well as being the energy that activates them.

If I'm correct in thinking that nonphysical energy—consciousness—directs our existence (I make no claims to infallibility), and if Maharishi and his literature do not explicitly acknowledge it, then this must be said about SCI: The chief theorist, Maharishi, seems to be "putting noise into the system" by making inconsistent statements as he attempts to translate his spiritual tradition into the language of science. This misdirection has led to the use of scientific-sounding language to describe SCI, supplying it with an air of respectability and credibility when there are really major flaws in the theory (and possibly the practice). This in turn has led to something other than truth in advertising, and, while it may be well intended, it's nevertheless propaganda, reflecting basic misunderstanding of and an infatuation with the glamor of science.

Which is too bad, really. Because the SCI literature reads so nicely.

Chapter 9

TM AND KUNDALINI

If India, the birthplace of TM, had eagerly embraced it, we might have reason to think that a truly revolutionary spiritual discipline had emerged upon the modern scene. But the plain fact is that India has just about ignored TM. It has been almost twenty years since Maharishi began his public teaching there. Yet, though some members of the Indian Parliament issued a statement in 1963 extolling Maharishi's system of TM and inviting people to become involved in the movement, today in that country of five hundred million there are only about forty thousand people practicing TM. Why is there such an apparent rejection of—or at least indifference to— TM in Maharishi's homeland?

The reason, in my opinion, is the Indian spiritual heritage. Because of it, Indians are hip to the fact that TM is beginner's meditation, that Maharishi is not as "high" as some of the holy men who have remained in India, and that there is more to enlightenment than Maharishi has told the public in the west.

What might that "more" be?

In October 1974, Dr. Karan Singh, India's Minister of Health, announced that the Indian government would conduct a long-range scientific study of yoga. The announcement was made to twenty-three hundred scientists gathered at the International Congress of Physiological

Sciences in New Delhi—eighteen hundred of whom came from abroad. The president of Maharishi International University, Dr. R. Keith Wallace, was among them.

Keith probably felt somewhat uncomfortable by the time the congress adjourned. He certainly was "quite disappointed," for he later told me this. After all, he had presented a talk entitled "The Neurophysiology of Enlightenment" in which he'd reviewed the scientific research on TM and said, "TM has revealed several important features of the nature of enlightenment and the processes through which it is gained." And the Indians hadn't bought it.

A few days after the congress, the eminent Indian meditation researcher Dr. B. K. Anand, who was studying yogis in samadhi when Keith was still in grade school, told the public that he and other scientists at the All-India Institute of Medical Sciences were planning to study kundalini yoga. "It is wrong to say Indian scientists have lagged behind in the study of yoga," the *Hindustan Times* reported Dr. Anand as saying. Then he dropped his bombshell. "The brain soothing effects of transcendental meditation have been noted by Indian physiologists in thousands of cases. But what should be studied now are the more intense yoga practices."

Brain soothing! In other words, he implied that TM may be good for relaxing you, for curing psychosomatic disorders, even for blissing you out—but don't think it's the key to enlightenment!

There can be no doubt about the extremely high significance that Indian scientists place on consciousness research. On another occasion, Dr. Karan Singh noted that a physiological study of intense yoga practices may be of "truly global significance" and that "the real thing to be investigated is the part played by yoga in the attainment of higher consciousness." The questions he raised in his address to the International Congress of Physiological Sciences in 1974 are most pertinent to our examination of TM and enlightenment, so I will quote him at length.

The link between the mind and the body is now being recognized, but the psychosomatic linkages are still imperfectly understood. . . . Man's predominant faculty is the capacity to be conscious of himself and his surroundings. What is the texture of this consciousness? What are the links between the genetic structure of man and his capacity for conscious awareness? Can manipulating the one influence the other? What are the functions of those areas of the brain that are still unexplored? Is man, in fact, evolving toward a transmutation of consciousness in much the same way as animal consciousness after millions of years on this planet evolved and developed into human consciousness? Is it possible that man is on the threshold of a new evolution? If so, what will be the concomitant changes required in the human body, particularly the brain?

These questions reveal the cosmic dimensions behind the study to be conducted at the All-India Institute of Medical Sciences. Research will focus on cases in which a yogi is reputed to have achieved higher brain functioning through the activation of *kundalini*.

Kundalini is a Sanskrit word meaning "coiled" like a snake or spring, and it is traditionally symbolized as a serpent. According to ancient Indian documents and modern seers, kundalini is a form of latent bioenergy in the human body—the body's basic life force—that can be concentrated in the brain to produce enlightenment and genius.

These ancient texts on kundalini, including some of those on which Maharishi bases TM, maintain that kundalini energy is present throughout the body, but that it is especially concentrated near the base of the spine in the region of the life-force-transmitting genitals. Through yoga disciplines, this "serpent energy" can be "awakened" and guided up the spine through various "chakras" or nerve centers to the brain. Extremely potent, this energy is said to be the key to raising consciousness for higher

mental perception, although it has not yet been identified
by science.

The All-India Institute's aim will be to test the kundalini concept and find out whether there is scientific cor-
roboration for the ancient literature. "The project," Dr.
Karan Singh said at a seminar on yoga, science, and man
in March 1975, "revolves particularly around the books
on kundalini by Pandit Gopi Krishna. These books are
arousing keen interest not only in India but throughout
the world. They present the stunning hypothesis that the
next step in human evolution will not be a physical development but a development in consciousness."

Who is this man, Gopi Krishna? Why doesn't Maharishi talk about kundalini if Indian spiritual tradition and
modern Indian scientists engaged in consciousness research see it as the key concept to investigate in seeking
to understand the nature of enlightenment?

Gopi Krishna is a yogi-scientist-philosopher, now in
his seventies, who lives in Srinagar, Kashmir. Gopi
Krishna and Maharishi met once, according to a story
I've heard—it happened in Srinagar in 1968. I haven't
been able to verify this yet, so I must say honestly that
at this point I'm reporting a rumor.

Be that as it may, the story goes like this: Maharishi
gave a public address about TM to some two thousand
people in Srinagar. He spoke for two hours, and when
he'd finished he asked if there were any questions or comments. Gopi Krishna was in the audience, and when he
raised his hand, he was invited to come to the platform.
He went to the microphone on stage and talked for fifteen
minutes. In that time he absolutely devastated Maharishi
and TM, saying that TM was a hypnotic technique of no
spiritual worth whatsoever.

Maharishi, so the story goes, was stunned and almost
speechless. He asked if that meant he had been hypnotiz-
ing himself into bliss all those years. "Exactly," was the
reply.

Some of Maharishi's devoted attendants urged him to
reply, so he asked for a meeting the next day. Gopi

Krishna agreed readily. However, Maharishi arrived at the meeting with a large entourage of disciples and devotees, thereby making it impossible to have an orderly debate.

In a gesture of good will, Gopi Krishna gave Maharishi a copy of his autobiography, *Kundalini*. And that, according to one of Gopi Krishna's friends, is when Maharishi got the idea for verifying TM scientifically, for Gopi Krishna had been calling on science to validate the claims of true yogis for years. Thus Gopi Krishna's friend feels that even though Maharishi doesn't acknowledge the existence of kundalini in public—he doesn't even admit to knowing the word—his whole concept of involving science in TM was ripped off from Gopi Krishna.

Regardless of the authenticity of this story, I now want to look at the subject of kundalini as Gopi Krishna presents it.

In 1937, at the age of thirty-four, Gopi Krishna experienced the awakening of kundalini. This was after seventeen years of intense and steadfast traditional yoga meditation in which he visualized a golden lotus opening at the top of his skull. He would get up every morning at 4 A.M. and meditate for several hours before going to work as a minor civil servant in the Indian government. In his autobiography, *Kundalini: The Evolutionary Energy in Man,* he writes, "There was a sound like a nerve thread snapping and instantaneously a silvery streak passed through the spinal cord, exactly like the sinuous movement of a white serpent in rapid flight, pouring an effulgent, cascading shower of brilliant energy into my brain, filling my head with a blissful luster. . . ."

Thus began the development of a higher state of consciousness within him. But remember what I said earlier about not mistaking bliss for enlightenment. The process begun that Christmas morning in 1937 was premature and far from complete. Because of it, there followed periods when Gopi Krishna's health deteriorated and his sanity was threatened by self-doubt and uncertainty. Because his physical and psychological pain became almost unbearable at times, desperation prompted him to begin observing his internal processes and experimenting carefully in the laboratory of his own body.

Now, after decades of mystical experience and with the development of psychic, intellectual, and literary powers, Gopi Krishna feels the process is complete and controlled. And a few years ago he decided to write about his life and research in order to enlist the aid of science in exploring the most important aspect of human life—the nature of enlightenment and the evolution of consciousness.

What does Gopi Krishna say specifically? He has explained his position in dozens of articles and in five books (four are listed in the "Suggested Readings" in the back of this book). Briefly, he claims that higher consciousness is the evolutionary goal of all humanity and that psychobiological transformation will harmonize the individual with society and with divine law.

Yoga and other spiritual disciplines, says Gopi Krishna, have been developed in every culture to support and speed up this evolutionary process. Their purpose is not merely to give aspirants peace of mind or a vision of God or psychic gifts, though these benefits do attend the process. Rather, true spiritual disciplines are designed to raise an ordinary person to the lofty stature of an intellectual prodigy, a genius, blessed with *vaikhari*—the spontaneous flow of words, either in poetry or prose, full of wisdom and value for others.

Sublimation of sex energy is the basic lever of all spiritual disciplines, Gopi Krishna said in a *New York Times* article on October 6, 1973. But "the all-inclusive nature of sex energy has not yet been correctly understood by psychologists. In fact, the very term reproductive, or sex, energy is a misnomer. Reproduction is but one of the aspects of the life energy, of which the other theater of activity is the brain."

Gopi Krishna is represented in America by the Kundalini Research Foundation in New York City. Mr. Gene Kieffer, president of the foundation, elaborated in a recent statement on the notion of life energy.

The most powerful motivating force of life, as Freud has shown, is sex and the pleasure drawn from the sexual act. Similarly, the most powerful motivating force to draw man onto the evolutionary path, according to the traditional concept of kundalini, is *ananda*. This highly extended state of consciousness, permeated with an extreme form of rapture, is said to be possible only when the consumption of *prana* is greatly enhanced. Prana is the bioplasma of living energy responsible for all vital activity of the body, including that of thought.

Mr. Kieffer adds that Gopi Krishna accepts no disciples, makes no demands for asceticism, and does not want to become the head of a cult or religious movement. Rather, he wants coworkers in the research he is pursuing. Most important of all, Gopi Krishna wants the truth of his observations about a potent biological link between sex and higher consciousness to be tested by trained scientists and scholars, using the principles and methodology of modern science. This is what the All-India Institute of Medical Sciences now plans to do.

Kundalini, the key word in Gopi Krishna's message, implies latent energy or potential for expansion. Gopi Krishna himself often translates it as "latent power-reservoir of energy" or "psychosomatic power center."

This fundamental bioenergy, as I have said, is stored primarily in the sex organs, but it permeates the entire body. Although normally associated with the genitals, where it provides sex drive (Freud called it libido), this potent "superintelligent electricity" is also the basis for attaining a higher state of consciousness, and its potency is our potential, Gopi Krishna says.

Kundalini may well be the evolutionary cause of creation as well as of procreation. As a link between sexual and spiritual experience, it may be the real "missing link" of human evolution.

Arousing the "serpent power" and guiding it up the spine to a dormant center in the brain is the goal of all spiritual and true occult disciplines, whether or not the practitioners recognize it as such, according to Gopi Krishna. When properly awakened, kundalini is the source of genius, psychic powers, artistic talent, scientific and intellectual genius—all characteristics of higher consciousness. (Gopi Krishna maintains, however, that these alone are not the full story. There is also a moral dimension to higher consciousness that is its primary characteristic and that distinguishes it from the consciousness of gifted psychics, intellectuals, etc. who are otherwise quite ordinary.)

Kundalini energy, when aroused, moves up the spinal cord through various "chakras" or nerve centers into the topmost chakra in the brain, which is located in the fourth ventricle (traditionally called the Cave of Brahma). During this process the entire nervous system—the body's link to universal consciousness—is transformed. The result is a new state of consciousness—cosmic consciousness.

Although kundalini is usually considered to be an Indian concept (there are thousands of ancient Vedic and tantric texts on the subject still untranslated into English), it is not discussed only in Hindu literature. Gopi Krishna's research has led him to conclude that evidence of kundalini exists in the ancient records of Tibet, Egypt, Sumer, China, Greece, and other cultures and traditions—including early Christianity. The Pharaoh's headdress, the feathered serpent of Mexico and South America, the serpent in the Garden of Eden—all are indicative of kundalini.

The source of the serpent power is *prana,* a primal cosmic energy outside the electromagnetic spectrum and all other force systems known to official science. Many traditions identify a life force from which other energies and paranormal phenomena are derived. As I have already mentioned, acupuncture calls it *ch'i;* the Greeks wrote of "ether;" Christianity terms it "the holy spirit;" Baron Karl von Reichenbach reported the discovery of "the odic force;" Wilhelm Reich named it "orgone;" Russian psychic researchers have their "bioplasma." And Carl Jung said that there are more than fifty synonyms for prana or *prima materia* in alchemical literature. Apparently these are all different labels for the same basic force that permeates living organisms and is the source of all vital activity, including thought, feeling, perception, and movement.

This vital essence, Gopi Krishna says, is extracted from surrounding organic tissue in the form of an extremely fine, highly delicate, volatile biochemical essence—concentrated prana. He has described it as a "psychic radiation" within the body, and he claims that whenever he and other highly developed yogis choose to "look within" themselves, they can directly observe the activity of this energy. In its immaterial form, as "cosmic prana," it allows them at times to see into the future.

How does one control and direct this energy? To learn to do so is the purpose of spiritual disciplines. Hatha yoga and raja yoga are among the oldest and most highly developed systems for raising the serpent power. But since "yoga" means "union with the divine," Gopi Krishna points out, *any* spiritual discipline that aims at attaining oneness with the Supreme Intelligence—not just at getting psychic powers or control over others—is a form of yoga.

Gopi Krishna adds a strong note of caution on the matter of attempting to awaken kundalini. The techniques for controlling it are extremely dangerous. Improperly performed, the kundalini process can be horribly painful and self-destructive. The "white light" experience of the mystics can become the "ugly glaring light" of a schizophrenic and the "signs and wonders" performed by saints can turn into psychic phenomena that terrify people who naïvely venture beyond the limits of their understanding and preparation. Without proper guidance from an adept teacher who knows the subtle workings of kundalini from personal experience, and without the right preparation— that is, a healthy, ethical, balanced manner of living— kundalini can become the source of deteriorating health, terrible bodily pain, many forms of mental illness and insanity, and even sudden death.

Kundalini gone astray, Gopi Krishna claims, has given rise to such evil geniuses as Hitler. In these cases the kundalini energy has been active since birth, as it is with all geniuses. Their lives, however, are usually fraught with difficulties, and the kundalini energy can become malignant if the finer qualities necessary for psychological stability have not been part of their upbringing. Since only the person who has active kundalini from birth is a potential Hitler, knowledge of kundalini is our best way of preventing another such as he.

Knowledge of kundalini is the only real path to preventing history from ending in nuclear holocaust, in psychic fascism, or in the slow death of an overpopulated, starving, resourceless planet. Gopi Krishna states: "The only way to safety and survival lies in determining evolutionary needs and in erecting our social and political systems in conformity with those needs." And he adds, "The awakening of kundalini is the greatest enterprise and most wonderful achievement in front of man."

If this was all Gopi Krishna had to say, it would be interesting but not compelling. Others have talked and written about kundalini before him. But Gopi Krishna—who makes it clear that he has only rediscovered an ancient tradition—is also a man of science. And in this respect, he says something that hasn't been said before—that kundalini can be scientifically verified in the laboratory. The presence of this evolutionary mechanism and energy in humans can be demonstrated clearly, using the methods and technology of science. We can obtain objective evidence that will show that the major claim of spiritual traditions throughout history—namely, that man was born to attain a higher state, a state of union with the divine—is true and real.

Gopi Krishna speaks with the authority of personal experience. His mission is to give us a sound understanding of kundalini through scientific and scholarly research. He wants to demystify and explain in clear, simple terms what is an occult matter in the ancient texts.

How might the reality of kundalini be shown? First, Gopi Krishna says, the person in whom kundalini is fully awakened will be a genius, no matter what his I.Q. was before the experience. This statement represents a radical departure from the prevailing view, which holds that intelligence is determined once and for all by the condition of the genes at birth. How to determine genius? The hallmark of it is *new* knowledge—knowledge such as Gopi Krishna himself offers, elegantly uniting the whole psychic-occult-spiritual scene of ancient traditions with Darwin's evolutionary theory and the transpersonal psychology arising from Freud, Jung, and Maslow.

Second, as the kundalini process transforms a person, his nervous system and brain undergo changes that will be observable—although the instruments necessary for observing the metamorphosis may still be on the drawing boards.

Next, since the "food" that the body uses to nourish the nervous system during this transformation comes from the sex organs—it is the "essence" of seminal fluid in men and what Gopi Krishna calls "the erotic fluids" in women —the reproductive organs will increase their activity dramatically, producing fluids many times more copiously than usual—sometimes to an embarrassing extent. (This, Gopi Krishna points out, explains those mysterious ancient paintings and statues that show men in meditation—even a pharaoh and one of the Egyptian gods—with erect penises. The artists did not mean these works to be erotic; rather, they are frank depictions of a biological fact about kundalini.)

This fluid essence, existing probably at the molecular or even atomic level, streams from the reproductive organs into the spinal canal and thence to the brain—a fact that can be verified, according to Gopi Krishna, by a spinal tap at the time the phenomenon is occurring.

During this organic transformation the bloodstream also carries nerve food. Hence the composition of the blood will change with the awakening of kundalini, and it ought to be examined in all research programs. Likewise, heart activity (pulse rate) and other internal organs undergo radical changes; perception, digestion, and elimination change dramatically. These changes can be clues to the full spectrum of physical-mental-behavioral transmutation that must necessarily occur as nature prepares the organism through a total cellular reorganization for a higher state of being, and these changes can be objectively determined by neurophysiologists and medical people.

Finally, since the person in whom kundalini is fully awakened will have high moral character and other traits (such as psychic and literary talents) typically associated with spiritual masters, psychologists and others will be able to identify him with tests for these traits.

This is a daring stance—daring, yet rationally and plausibly presented by Gopi Krishna. Gopi Krishna is making a breathtaking attempt to heal the split between science and religion by offering the first *testable* field theory of psychophysiological relationships between mind, body, and cosmos. His conception of kundalini covers the entire spectrum of psychological, psychic, and spiritual phenomena, and with it comes the possibility of objectively studying higher consciousness. Such objective study would end metaphysical speculation and endless claim-and-counterclaim arguments among various sects and traditions about whose leader or guru is "highest."

In the past, great mystics and saints spoke of enlightenment in figurative language based on sexual images; they said that sexual images were the closest they could come to describing otherwise indescribable experiences. Conventional psychology has tended to dismiss this as repressed sexuality, but it now appears there may be a biological basis for such imagery—a definite physical link between body and mind, between sexual and spiritual experience. From the viewpoint of transpersonal psychology, one could say that *sexuality is really unexpressed or unfulfilled religious experience.* It is humorously ironic that western science and technology—often called the product of a godless, materialistic approach to life—might be the means by which this is demonstrated to the world.

If Gopi Krishna is a man to whom attention should be given, is TM doing any research along the lines he suggests? The answer is no. As of October 1975, when I inquired at the International Center for Scientific Research in Los Angeles (the clearing house for TM research), there was absolutely nothing to report. In part, this is because official policy discourages comparing TM with other techniques such as kundalini yoga. I think this is unfortunate—a small part of the vast research facilities and funds at SIMS' disposal might very profitably be directed into kundalini research. Are there reasons for avoiding the term and the topic that TM people do not publicly state?

For whatever it's worth, my opinion on the matter is that kundalini is *the* most important area for science to examine, bar none, and that of those who address themselves to this awesome subject, Gopi Krishna speaks most sensibly, pragmatically, and comprehensively. This shouldn't be taken as an endorsement of him personally— I've never met him or even corresponded with him. I merely want to go on record as recognizing the importance of what he has to say. And now I'll let him have the last word on kundalini:

> The aim of this evolutionary impulse is to make man aware of himself, and with this sublime awareness, to make him regulate his life as a rational human being, free from egotism, violence, excessive greed and ambition and immoderate lust and desire, to lead to a state of unbroken peace and happiness on the earth. . . .
>
> Enlightenment, therefore, is a natural process ruled by biological laws as strict in their operation as the laws governing the continuance of the race. The central target of this evolution is self-awareness for the soul. . . . This is the purpose for which you and I are here—to realize ourselves . . . to bring the soul to a clear realization of its own divine nature.

Chapter 10

WHAT IS HIGHER CONSCIOUSNESS?

Many false gods have arisen among us in recent times. Spiritual hustlers abound. The public is being exposed to claims and counterclaims from people who are said (often by self-proclamation) to be in higher consciousness. Higher than what, though? And just what *is* higher consciousness? Let's not be taken in by vague claims, mystifying rhetoric, and lavish advertising campaigns. Instead, let's demand that people sporting the title of spiritual leader or holy man present their credentials for security.

In order to evaluate credentials, I'll try in this chapter to give you a sort of checklist for judging who's enlightened and who's not. I hope it gives you some tools for tuning up your "spiritual crap detector" so that the ignorant, the deluded, the charlatans, and the psychopaths can be seen for what they are.

Before we go any further in our examination of higher consciousness, however, we should ask ourselves one very important question: What is consciousness?

Consciousness isn't the same thing as thinking, because we can be aware of our thoughts—thoughts take place within consciousness and are thereby secondary to it. We can also be aware without having any thoughts—only perceptions. You've probably had a moment in which you gaze blankly at a spot without thinking anything, just passively experiencing what's happening, as if in a daze.

This shows that perceptions, too, are secondary to the field of awareness in which they occur.

Many things can be learned about *the contents of consciousness*—thoughts, perceptions, feelings, values, beliefs, memories, related physiological processes, and so forth. The organization of these contents into a recognizable configuration is what we call psyche or mind; you may have heard someone say, "I know his mind well."

But consciousness itself, the basic act of being aware, is the means by which we know whatever it is that we know. Consciousness is primary, and it can't be explained in terms of anything else—it can only be experienced. Without consciousness, no observations or experiences are in any way possible.

There are three senses in which people use the word "consciousness." First, it means simple awareness within an organism—the capacity for perceiving and feeling. In this sense, animals display consciousness. But animals don't display personal self-awareness, the conscious (as opposed to the nonconscious, animal-like) aspect of mind reflecting an *abstract concept* or image of oneself. In other words, animals don't display ego. This uniquely human trait is the second sense in which we can answer the question "What is consciousness?" It is awareness of yourself as a separate being and the subsequent identification with some aspect of your being—your body, your mind, your achievements, etc.

The third sense in which "consciousness" is used takes us beyond the physical body. Since psychic research has demonstrated that telepathy, clairvoyance, precognition, psychokinesis, and out-of-body travel are real phenomena,* there must be some means through which the connection between physically separate objects and events can be made. That "connection" is consciousness as the universal field in which all experience and/or awareness occurs. Maharishi uses the terms "Being" and "field of Being" as synonyms for consciousness in this sense.

* Edgar D. Mitchell's *Psychic Exploration* (New York: G. P. Putnam's Sons, 1974) offers a good survey of psychic research.

Although we can distinguish meanings, we can't really define consciousness. To define is to limit, to set boundaries—and who knows where consciousness begins or ends? Certainly animals are conscious (but not self-conscious). Neurophysiologists talk of "spinal consciousness" in lower animals; biologists note the "protoplasmic consciousness" of protists, single-celled creatures lacking nervous systems. Polygraph expert Cleve Backster opened a new window on consciousness—though it is much disputed—when he and others claimed to have observed "primary perception" in cellular life. (This began with his famous report on perception in plants. Later he reported finding sentience in single cells of blood, yeast, paramecia, and even semen.)

Apparently, then, wherever life is, consciousness is. Tie that in with exobiology, which suggests the probability of other life forms in the universe, and we can say that since there are stellar systems significantly older than ours, it is likely that some life forms are more highly evolved than *homo sapiens.* Shall we call such entities forms of higher consciousness? Why not?

Some religious and philosophic traditions—Maharishi's is one—hold that all creation, even so-called inorganic matter, possesses a primal form of sentience or awareness. From their points of view, consciousness is everywhere—it is the foundation of all existence, the organizing principle behind the physical universe.

We can't define consciousness, yet every day's living confirms its reality. We are conscious, and consciousness is the self-evident dimension of all knowing, all perception, all states of being. Whatever happens on the spectrum of our physical and mental life—waking, sleeping dreaming, making love, getting high, feeling low, hungry or happy—is an alteration in or disturbance of consciousness. And on the basis of recent psychic research, even death is now apparently an altered state of consciousness after death, consciousness continues in a noncorporeal o: discarnate condition.

The boundaries of personal awareness constantly shif like changing images on a movie screen, and, with them our perceptions, abilities, and understanding of reality shift. Reflection leads to an awareness of awareness—an expansion of consciousness, if you will—and also to the possibility, long maintained by many traditions, of integrating the conscious and unconscious aspects of mind to develop a new and stable state of awareness, the ultra-conscious—or, as it has also been called, cosmic consciousness, samadhi, satori, or mystical union.

The range of psychic, paranormal, and mystic experiences being investigated today is bewildering to the general public, and consciousness researchers themselves often seem to be confused too. The unfamiliar terrain is being mapped in ways that aren't always congruent, and many "authorities," upon becoming aware of higher levels in the spectrum of consciousness, have been humbled by the depth of experience systematized in spiritual traditions.

Let's be clear about something from the start. Our knowledge of higher consciousness comes from two classes of people—saints and mystics—and this is one of the major points of confusion in the field of consciousness research. These two types of explorers in the spiritual stratosphere often aren't distinguished from one another, but mystics aren't necessarily saints, and vice versa. Mystics know primarily through the head, saints through the heart. (The *truly* enlightened, though, have always been saintly mystics or mystical saints—integrated people knowing fully through both modes.)

There is an important difference between mystical and mystifying, incidentally. The latter kind of people try to dazzle you with their verbal footwork, perhaps throwing in some psychic phenomena to doubly impress you and cultivating an air of inscrutability. But these are all ego games, and those who puzzle and those who amaze might be anything but enlightened. Jesus' test of higher consciousness still stands—by their fruits ye shall know them. All a person's claims and verbiage and spectacular displays don't mean much unless his manner of living gives evidence of an enlightened mind working for the liberation of mentally enslaved, suffering people. Purpose, meaning, direction in life—that's what people need and are searching for most of all, however ignorantly. And that's what the enlightened try to help others find.

Adolf Hitler is perhaps the best example of a mystic who was not a saint. Several important books have recently given us a radically revised and important new portrait of Hitler. In *The Occult Reich, The Occult and the Third Reich,* and, most important of all, *The Spear of Destiny,* clear, strong documentation of the occult foundations of the Nazi movement are presented. These books convincingly propose that Hitler was a mystic of sorts whose inner circle of supporters were occultists practicing black magic and had considerable knowledge about altered states of consciousness. Hitler's high native intelligence—and from Gopi Krishna's point of view, active kundalini—were raised to near-genius level through personal experience of transcendent consciousness, gained primarily through use of psychedelic drugs such as peyote and through initiation into occult practices for expanding awareness.

These mind-expanding experiences Hitler had as a young man gave him sporadic access to an illumined state that later led him to say to one of his generals, "The purpose of human life is to gain a mystic view of the universe." This is a surprising statement, far out of keeping with the stereotyped, one-dimensional image of Hitler historians have thus far given us. It shows deep affinity with the thought of evolutionists such as Teilhard de Chardin, Sri Aurobindo, Gopi Krishna, R. M. Bucke, Oliver Reiser, and others.

Hitler's evolutionary notion of the super-race was formed not so much through reading philosophers such as Nietzsche as it was from direct experience of higher consciousness. But if der Führer had a significant degree of mystical understanding, he failed woefully to develop it in a balanced, integrated way, and thus—quite obviously!—failed to develop saintly character traits. Malignant internal and external influences distorted his inner vision and genius. Psychopathology developed, leading—

unfortunately for humanity—to the holocaust of World War II.

Mystics bring us new knowledge of higher consciousness; saints demonstrate it in their lives. Mystics don't necessarily have the loving, selfless qualities of saints, but saints don't necessarily have the intellectual capacity or theoretical understanding that they need to translate their awareness into terms that verbally communicate their experiences with depth and precision.

What mystics and saints *do* have in common is experience of the higher self, of a state in which the bonds of ego are dissolved or demolished or perceived as illusion. In this state the narrow view of self and world that ego creates is transcended for the moment and a larger, more fundamental sense of self-as-cosmos emerges into awareness, accompanied by an experience of peace, deep understanding of the nature of existence, and the perception of white light.

But one white-light experience does not a mystic make. It is only the beginning of a lifelong journey. *The exploration of higher consciousness never ceases,* our sages, seers, and saviors tell us, *and enlightenment is an endless process.* True, there are quantum leaps in awareness that mark certain stages of growth on the spiritual path. But the path that leads to God who is our home wanders all over the universe—indeed, it leads through the interpenetrating universes, the successional multiverses, the infinity of omniverses. One lifetime is sufficient to reach enlightenment, but not to complete it, for the cosmic adventure is forever. Death is only a transition marking the end of one round in the evolution of consciousness and the beginning of another.

I might add that Hitler's statement was wrong—or at least not fully correct. The purpose of human life is not simply to gain a mystic view of the universe; it is to gain that view *and then lovingly share it with others.* Service to humanity in the name of divinity should be a primary guideline as we check out an individual's enlightenment status. We're looking for saintly mystics or mystical saints—not to worship them, but to learn from them and revere them—and we shouldn't settle for less.

We've seen that consciousness is the primary dimension of our being. Now we can say that *higher consciousness is the unification of personal awareness on all levels with universal consciousness.* It is a transformation of one's total being—both inner state and outer behavior. The ego—a mental structure that holds in check our human potential for growth in all aspects of consciousness—is swept away, and that new sense of self-as-cosmos pervades awareness. Some traditions call this illumination; others call it enlightenment or cosmic consciousness. Its essence is a self-transforming realization of one's total union with the infinite beyond time and space. As the *Maitrayana Upanishad* puts it: "Having realized his own self as the Self, a man becomes selfless. . . . This is the highest mystery."

Consciousness manifests itself in four primary mental qualities—intelligence, will, perception, and feeling. Any mental trait or event, it seems to me, can finally be categorized under one or more of these four basic aspects of mind. If my analysis is correct, higher consciousness involves intensifying and refining these qualities. Let's consider each briefly.

Intelligence has always been a hallmark of enlightened individuals. Isn't that why we call then "spiritual geniuses"? Their I.Q.s haven't been measured, so far, but we can presume that when they are, they'll come out in the high percentiles. (One I.Q. expert estimated Martin Luther's at 170.) That's not the point, though—the point is that spiritual geniuses have applied their high native intelligence in creative ways, have demonstrated that they possess *new* knowledge (for their time). And in support of their spiritual discoveries or inventions (such as an innovative meditational technique or spiritual exercise), they frequently demonstrate all the qualities of mind traditionally associated with genius in the ordinary sense. They have a good grasp of their tradition's history. They are familiar with holy scripture and wisdom literature of other traditions. They are articulate and even eloquent, with prodigious memory, razor-keen discrimination, and excellent ability to analyze. They also have the ability to think logically and calculate rapidly—not necessarily mathematically, but at the very least they can figure out problems quickly and make their ways nimbly through perplexing situations that boggle others. Consider, for example, the various snares set for Jesus by his enemies, and how he overcame them without a moment's hesitation. He was a real "street fighter" who could think on his feet.

Higher consciousness doesn't bestow all knowledge. There are many answers still to be learned. But it does bring wisdom based on character and spiritual growth. It also brings the patience to wait for answers instead of filling the void by sacrificing intellectual integrity and leaping into simple-minded or irrational belief. The enlightened don't believe—they *know*.

Will, another characteristic of the enlightened person, is a sometimes amazing quality. We are familiar with the will to win, the will to live, and so forth. People recognized as having higher consciousness usually show great will power. And this isn't sheer stubbornness—rather, in conjunction with intelligence, it is steadfast determination. This quality holds the enlightened person steadily on course throughout a multitude of changes in outward circumstances, some of which might overwhelm a lesser person. Will is the source of apparently superhuman strength against enormous difficulties.

What is it that those in higher consciousness have willed? First and foremost, to know God. Since changing consciousness is the name of the cosmic game, the ultimate action is no action at all except to focus your consciousness steadily on knowing God. Outward changes of dress, habits, diet, etc. are of value *if* they are consciously performed with the intention of aiding awareness development. (Indeed, the American seeking to raise his or her consciousness *should* make such changes, for our diet is so detrimental to good physical and mental health and our concern with fashion, style, and trend is so superficial that our spiritual development will be hampered unless we forsake these "all-American" things.) Without the willed intent to know God, however, changes in lifestyle are meaningless formalisms, empty ritual, mindless repetition of someone else's trip.

If a person wills himself to know God through *all* his activities, it seems to me that it really doesn't make much difference what sort of activities they are when he begins. We all have aspects of our lives that seem contrary to or unsupportive of unification with universal consciousness, and we can call these aspects "unspiritual" or "anti-enlightenment." But since the thing that really matters is what you *will*, these aspects of personal behavior will be eliminated naturally as insight deepens, and where social circumstances seem anti-spiritual, you will seek to transform them. (That's what karma yoga is all about.)

Perception can be sensory or extrasensory, and the latter is certainly a feature of higher consciousness. I imagine you've heard your share of miracle stories about yogis appearing in their astral bodies to prevent suicides or to give important messages to disciples telepathically or to read someone's aura and diagnose his health.

But let's not overlook the use of *normal* senses as employed by higher consciousness. How often a peak experience takes the form of one's simply becoming aware for the first time of the beauty and grandeur of the world! Zen training seeks in part to enhance such awareness—to cleanse the doors of perception so that the glory of here and now can be experienced. To see what actually is, to hear without preconception, to experience life with full sensory awareness is, all sources agree, an integral aspect of higher consciousness.

Finally, *feeling*—serenity, equanimity, tranquility, a state of calm joy beyond the heights and depths of raw emotion and desire—is a traditional hallmark of those in higher consciousness. Self-pity, fear, lust, jealousy, greed, and other negative emotions are rooted in ego, but enlightenment purges them from the mind through self-knowledge, and when they have been purged the positive emotions, such as compassion and courage (which are generally socially conditioned into quiescence), come to the fore. At this stage of enlightenment the capacity for feeling exquisite sensations is undimmed, but the passion that most people have to feel them is broken. The capacity for feeling with others—sympathy—is also undimmed, but in higher consciousness, feelings are refined to act in concert with intelligence and perception. As a result, sympathy never degenerates to pitying or pampering another, or to feeding the ego of the sympathizer. There is a saying that applies here: Feeling without truth is sentimentality, but truth without feeling is brutality.

Because they have cleared out the intellectual and emotional programming that leads to brutality and sentimentality, those in higher consciousness have learned the final lesson that transforms superior intelligence into true genius—*the enlightened, though different, are nevertheless just like everyone else.* Beneath the superficial differences of appearance and talent, we are all human becomings, still babes in the cosmic woods. Humility is the only proper response to enlightenment.

To help define enlightenment further, let's look at some definitions of higher consciousness that can serve as guidelines for "gauging the guru." The first I can offer comes from Dr. Haridas Chaudhuri, who was introduced in Chapter 7. "Enlightenment," said Dr. Chaudhuri in an interview printed in *Synthesis* (vol. 1, no. 2, 1975), "means not only expansion of consciousness and broadening of horizons, but also deep inner value-consciousness. No matter how much [psychic] power a person may have, he may still be a devil's disciple if his value-consciousness has not been purified. This is the essence of spiritual realization: value-consciousness. Otherwise there is always the danger of exploiting power for self-aggrandizement."

Dr. Chaudhuri's experience was primarily in the yogic tradition. Another modern master, Lama Govinda, speaks from the Tibetan Buddhist tradition to affirm the same view of enlightenment. *Human Dimensions* magazine (vol. 4, no. 2, 1975) printed his view in an article entitled "Consciousness Expansion Versus Consciousness Intensification."

... The mere expansion of a muddled consciousness, in which the faculties of discrimination, mental
balance, and understanding have not yet been developed, does not constitute an improvement and will
not lead to the attainment or the realization of a
higher dimension of consciousness, but only to a
worse confusion, to an expansion of ignorance and
an indiscriminate involvement in irrelevant impressions and emotions. Therefore, a wise person would
rather follow the advice of the great spiritual leaders
and benefactors of humanity by concentrating his
mind and improving its quality, instead of trying to
expand it without rhyme or reason, i.e., without having developed the faculty of understanding or discrimination.

Enlightenment, according to these men, is characterized
by (1) commitment based on personal experience to the
time-tested value of selfless service which is the heart of
every spiritual tradition, (2) a fine sense of discrimination, (3) mental balance, and (4) deep insight.

A comment by Gandhi defines the perfect yogi of action, the karma yogi. "He is a devotee who is jealous of
none, who is a fount of mercy, who is without egotism,
who is selfless, who treats alike cold and heat, happiness
and misery, who is ever forgiving, who is always con-
tented, whose resolutions are firm, who has dedicated
mind and soul to God, who causes no dread, who is not
afraid of others, who is free from exultation, sorrow, and
fear, who is pure, who is versed in action yet remains
unaffected by it, who renounces all fruit [of actions], good
or bad, who treats friend and foe alike, who is untouched
by respect or disrespect, who is not puffed up by praise,
who does not go under when people speak ill of him,
who loves silence and solitude, who has a disciplined
reason. Such devotion is inconsistent with the existence
at the same time of strong attachments."

Higher consciousness is a term that can easily be mis-
applied. Certainly it includes the flashes of illumination

that many have in varying degrees, but those peak experiences, though invaluable and essential, are not the final integration of the adult personality.

Peak experiences often come unbidden, but they are only a call to transformation, an invitation to "work on yourself" further. The goal is to achieve a stable plateau experience of constant illumination expressed through balanced character; this requires dedicated application through honest self-examination, cultivation of the mind, refinement of the character, and service to the world.

As you begin to grow in awareness and to experience different levels of being, many wonders and terrors may await you, and the person of discrimination will attempt to understand them without succumbing to them through fascination (if they're wondrous) or fear (if they're terrifying). Meeting angels and demons is a well-reported phenomenon among those who have penetrated to the supersensible realms. The Swedish mystic Emanuel Swedenborg had this to say about his experience with the elementals:

> When spirits begin to speak with a man, he must beware that he believe nothing that they say. For nearly everything they say is fabricated by them, and they lie—for if they are permitted to narrate anything, as what heaven is and how things in the heavens are to be understood, they would tell so many lies that a man would be astonished. This they would do with solemn affirmation. . . . Wherefore men must beware and not believe them. . . .

Other soul travelers agree with Swedenborg. Don't get sidetracked and don't settle for second best. Test your visions. They're first cousins to fantasy and hallucination. Try to believe as little as possible and *know* as much as possible. Use your intelligence, your will, your perceptions, and your feelings honestly and truthfully to test your sense of reality and stay on course, because there are many pitfalls along the way. Jesus put the matter simply when he said, "Thou shalt love the Lord thy God with all thy heart [feeling], and with all thy soul [perception], and with all thy mind [intelligence], and with all thy strength [will]."

There are no quick courses in higher consciousness, no guaranteed methods, no gurus who can hand it to you with a touch or a word. The most they can do is awaken your own longing for an expanded state. Some are quite skillful at this, and when they do it lovingly, selflessly, they are to be gratefully appreciated. But the evolution of consciousness is always endless, always your own responsibility. Since most people have never lived outside the spiritual equivalent of the Kansas flatlands, it's relatively easy to induce a slight opening-up in them, a minor peak experience. For them, a short drive along the spiritual equivalent of, say, the Mohawk Trail through the Massachusetts Berkshires is thrilling, breathtaking, the sort of experience that motivates them to describe it lavishly in letters to the folks back home.

But if you seek higher peak experiences, you've got to learn mountain climbing. A drive through the Berkshires, where you can safely stop and get out at well-known scenic vistas, is fine. But you don't see the real glories of nature that way. To do so, you need mountain-climbing equipment and an experienced guide.

And you have to "learn the ropes." With the basic know-how, you'll gradually prepare yourself to enter the Rockies. The dangers and difficulties there are much greater, however, and few from the flatlands can say they've made it all the way up the Great Divide. Skill, fortitude, and endurance are required.

Beyond the Rockies are the Himalayas. Beyond the highest peak experiences are the plateau experiences that can only be known by those who deliberately train themselves to live at the top of the world as members of that small community of spiritual explorers who can be said to be permanently in higher consciousness.

It's an ardous journey, they tell us, but the view is entirely worth the climb. If you wish to begin, know that the Berkshires, the Rockies, and the Himalayas are all within you, no matter where you find yourself physically located on the planet. There is no need to leave home, no need to hurry toward enlightenment, because you're already there, potentially. You just haven't realized it, actualized it.

Often you can see people whose behavior desperately says, "I *must* get enlightened." Others proclaim with spiritual pride that their last meditation knocked off at least eighty karma points and three reincarnations. Such people are spiritually blind to the fact that *enlightenment is here and now*. Open your eyes and see the wonder of God's world. The journey is the teaching. The ordinary is extraordinary. Enjoy it. In Zen there is a saying that goes like this: "Before I came to Zen, mountains were only mountains, rivers only rivers, trees only trees. After I got into Zen, mountains were no longer mountains, rivers no longer rivers, trees no longer trees. But when enlightenment happened, mountains were again only mountains, rivers again only rivers, trees again only trees."

Reality is reality. The only difference is that, in higher consciousness, you'll relate to it in a new way. As a wise yogi once said, there's nothing wrong with the world except your attitude toward it. From wrong attitudes—that is, from *ignorant* attitudes—spring all evil and suffering.

What is an attitude? It's a habitual way of processing information, a habitual mode of experiencing life. We're all creatures of habit, but are your habits unconsciously conditioned or freely chosen? Spiritual disciplines are designed to help you choose them freely through deep self-knowledge.

So take an attitude check—and remember that the ultimate action is no action at all except to center your consciousness on knowing God, the Tao, ultimate reality. This, incidentally, explains why the Greek word *metanoia,* used in the Bible centuries ago to describe the conversion experience, doesn't mean "repentance" in the ordinary sense of being sorry for something you did. Poor translation of that word has led to a degeneration of the Biblical message in this respect. Rightly understood, metanoia (which literally means "going beyond the ordinary mind state") indicates a change of mind and heart based on deep insight into your personal behavior.

Metanoia really means "a new state of awareness" or "a new state of consciousness." To get to metanoia, consciousness researcher John Lilly points out, you have to move from orthonoia, the ordinary mind state, through paranoia, a state of derangement and rearrangement of the psyche, in order to demolish the ego, and that's when those mountains, rivers, and trees can seem so strange. But, as Lord Krishna said to Arjuna—"Fare forward fearlessly, voyager."

Chapter 11

IS MAHARISHI ENLIGHTENED?

Judge not, lest ye be judged, the Bible warns us. I agree completely, and as I understand that admonition, it means stop all the moralistic, self-righteous condemnation and ego games that make you think you're superior to everyone else. It does *not* mean to cease discerning, discriminating, and evaluating. To refrain from these processes would be to surrender our God-given intelligence.

To those who will think I'm *judging* Maharishi with this chapter, I reply that I'm attempting to *assess* him. That may seem to be the height of presumption because I've never met him (although I'd certainly like to); but I feel that I have some useful information about and insights into the man behind TM, gained from talking with people who do know him and who have spent time in training with him, and I want to share these.

Is Maharishi enlightened? I'll answer straight from the shoulder—yes and no.

That's *not* meant to be evasive doubletalk. Enlightenment is an endless process, and even in unity consciousness there is always lots more to learn (especially about living spiritually *in community,* which is something that TM has little to say about). In fact, lately Maharishi has been privately mentioning a state of consciousness *beyond* unity—Brahma consciousness.

We can certainly credit Maharishi with a degree of

illumination, at least tentatively, while still recognizing that he may be of lesser stature than spiritual giants of the past and of the present day. From one point of view, Maharishi can be seen as carrying out the highest yogic tradition. This tradition requires that the self-realized yogi, the one who has withdrawn from the world in order to seek enlightenment, *return* to society to help other struggling souls attain liberation. In *The Psychobiology of Transcendental Meditation,* Kanellakos and Lukas quote from a letter Maharishi sent to them that deals with precisely this point:

It is commonly understood that people who take to the meditative life, like monks, become introverted and avoid activity; they don't seem to participate in the progress of civilization. The tendency of this type of life shows in the deleterious effects on the physiology of its practitioners. Such people, who use wrong systems of meditation, neither contribute their best to society nor do they derive the joy of life from the advances made in civilization.

Only an enlightened person, who has no attachments, no karma, no worldliness to corrupt his mission, can truly help suffering souls in the world. Such a person is *in* the world but not *of* it, operating within social conventions and institutions but not bound by them.

Outwardly, Maharishi seems to be living up to this ideal. I know of no scandal attached to him such as those that have tainted the images of Guru Maharaj-ji (who has been publicly charged with playboy living and has engaged in courtroom fights over movement leadership), Swami Satchidananda (who has been publicly charged with breaking his yogic vow of celibacy), Sun Myung Moon (who has been publicly charged with brainwashing disciples and encouraging them to lie), and others.

In fairness, then, we must acknowledge the possibility that Maharishi and the TM movement leaders are sincerely and intelligently acting out of love for humanity; that their "product" isn't merely a hypnotic technique for thought control but rather is one that will live up to its claims about stimulating intelligence, creativity, and bliss; and that those claims for TM are in line with the evolutionary imperative to grow in consciousness.

Yet some critics of TM see a contradiction in Maharishi between his words and his actions. Maharishi says he is a renunciate, owning nothing, desiring nothing, but clearly he means for others to fully enjoy the world, materiality and all. And renunciate or not, he himself gets the best care money can buy, to the degree that he wishes. It's even been rumored—and it's strictly a rumor, as far as I know—that he can't go home because the Indian equivalent of the IRS wants a "look at the book" to see if he's been evading taxes on the millions of dollars that the TM movement, if not Maharishi personally, is worth.

Certainly Maharishi is a shrewd merchant—or, as one of his own people said, an "Armenian rug dealer." When the campus of Parsons College came up for sale, it looked "right" for Maharishi International University, so Maharishi stepped into the negotiations and beat the price down from fourteen million dollars to two and a half million. This sort of slick behavior in the money department has raised a lot of eyebrows.

Well, *is* TM a sophisticated hustle, as some skeptically declare, or is Maharishi showing seasoned, pragmatic wisdom eminently suited to the modern world's temperament? Is his "packaging" of meditation a brilliant simplification necessary for wide acceptance by the masses so that they, in their own time, can come to self-realization? Or is TM a debasement of the noblest spiritual traditions? Is Maharishi really a prophet who intends to use America —to which the rest of the world looks in almost every way except spiritually—to bring spiritual awareness to all humanity? Or is TM merely a subtle ploy to mask his true intention, which is grossly commercial and possibly a path to spiritual fascism? The answers to these questions depend on whether you think Maharishi is truly enlightened.

"Enlightenment" is a word that pops up frequently

now in everyday conversation and in the literature dispensed by TM people. Its increased usage can be attributed to Maharishi's proclamation on January 12, 1975 that the age of enlightenment had begun. Amid fanfare and ceremony at his Swiss headquarters, and under the motto "Through the window of science we see the dawn of the age of enlightenment," he announced to the world:

When I reviewed the information of the scientific research, I found that I should have done this three years ago. . . . But it doesn't matter; we are being dragged by the time. The Age of Enlightenment is dragging us on, and it's going to drag the whole world. It's going to take the world out of the darkness of the age of ignorance. On this dragging influence of time is our strength in inaugurating the Age of Enlightenment today.

The master of ceremonies at the inaugural celebration was Dr. R. Keith Wallace, president of Maharishi International University. In his opening remarks, Keith described enlightenment as follows:

The state of enlightenment represents the ultimate development of what we ordinarily consider to be the most valuable qualities of human life. Enlightenment results from the full development of consciousness and depends upon the perfect and harmonious functioning of every part of the body. What is unique today is that, first, the most ancient science for the development of consciousness has been re-established in its purest and most effective form by Maharishi Mahesh Yogi as the Science of Creative Intelligence. Second, it is being expressed in a way that makes it fully accessible to modern scientific techniques of investigation. The benefit of this meeting of the ancient and modern sciences is that enlightenment is now taken out of the realm of mysticism and uncertainty and shown to be a specific reality—verifiable, universally available, and of immense practical value. The process of refinement is completely natural, for it utilizes the existing mechanics of human physiology. The process of the development of enlightenment is open to anyone, starting from any level of consciousness, not requiring any specific life-style or system of belief. The ability to gain enlightenment is innate in the physiology of every human being, and, therefore, every human being deserves the knowledge of how to utilize it. As Maharishi has said, "There's no reason in our scientific age for anyone to remain unenlightened."

If your crap detector is functioning at all, its needle must have been jumping back and forth as those words were fed through. And some statements should have shot the needle way into the red section marked "Danger— nonsense," though others are in perfect agreement with the core truths of the world's major spiritual traditions.

Let's look at some of the main ideas in Keith's statement. If they're in error, it seems fair to say that they reflect directly on Maharishi. Few people are closer to him than Keith, who in addition to heading Maharishi International University is one of the five World Plan Executive Council directors (see the glossary in this book for a definition of WPEC). And any definition of enlightenment such as this one, which was publicly issued on a major occasion, is obviously intended for wide dissemination and use. Surely it has the imprimatur of Maharishi, so to speak—Keith wouldn't dare dispense such a *pronunciamento* without first getting the seal of approval.

Start with this. "Enlightenment is now taken out of the realm of mysticism and uncertainty. . . ." It certainly is —but not in the way Keith intended! What Keith *should* have said is that enlightenment is now taken out of the realm of *mystery* or *mystification,* for what is mystifying isn't necessarily mystical; it can be sheer nonsense presented in a puzzling way. For Keith to confuse these terms is not just a matter of linguistic imprecision. It shows a basic misunderstanding—a misunderstanding that says: Mysticism has not been understood until now.

And if that misunderstanding is the ground upon which Keith now defines enlightenment, it certainly *does* take enlightenment out of the realm of mysticism, where it has always dwelled and always will. It puts enlightenment in the realm of opinion and speculation and covers it with a veneer of scientific data—some of it now disputed—that in any case comes from subjects exhibiting no signs whatsoever of the traditional and well-understood characteristics of higher consciousness. But the plain truth is that enlightenment *cannot* be taken out of the realm of mysticism and that the most science can do is verify the long-known and clear fact that mystics are operating on a qualitatively higher level of mentality than the general population. If Maharishi and his followers think otherwise, I can only say that there's something fishy about their thinking.

How *do* mystics achieve their higher level of mental operation, anyway? According to Keith's statement, "Enlightenment results from the full development of consciousness and depends upon the perfect and harmonious functioning of every part of the body." But who has *ever* established a yardstick to measure the "full development of consciousness"? This kind of talk assumes that there is one measurement that applies to everyone, and that when you're enlightened it's like passing "Go." In a sense that analogy is appropriate, because the moment of entry into cosmic consciousness is a moment of radical departure from ordinary waking consciousness. But even in normal consciousness people may have hints and foreshadowings of cosmic consciousness during peak experiences that may be anything from orgasms to rare kinds of drug experiences. And passing "Go" is by no means the end, as I've pointed out before. Traditionally, entering cosmic consciousness has been likened to a baby's being born—even after a quantum leap in awareness there are whole new stages of growth to undergo. Furthermore, growth never ceases. As I said, enlightenment is an endless process.

And what about the idea that enlightenment "depends on the perfect and harmonious functioning of every part of the body"? Enlightenment, in other words, is a mental gift dependent upon the condition of the physical body, upon a perfect physical body? Never mind that this is a reductionist-materialist view, quite out of keeping with the traditional Vedic doctrine that reality is essentially spiritual or mental in nature. If we accept Keith's statement for the moment, must we assume that it rules out enlightenment for amputees? And what about the deaf or the blind? Is enlightenment out of the question for them too? If Keith is right about the need for a perfectly functioning body, presumably a polio victim with withered limbs and a bad heart couldn't reach enlightenment. What about a severely retarded person?

There seems to be a further contradiction between this part of Keith's statement and the part that says, "The process of the development of enlightenment is open to anyone, starting from any level of consciousness. . . ." TM teachers *know* that they can't teach their technique to the mentally retarded and the severely disturbed. (And remember that Dr. Otis' research, mentioned in Chapter 6, indicates that it *shouldn't* be taught to high-anxiety people.)

We must accept the fact that people differ widely in mental and physiological readiness for enlightenment. Whether these differences are due to some organic (perhaps genetically governed) cause or whether (in accordance with Maharishi's tradition) those differences are spiritual in origin and have to do with reincarnation, it's clear that there are parameters outside which one can't expect enlightenment to occur.

The situation is complex, of course, and you can certainly find examples of enlightened or at least highly evolved people whose bodily condition is (or was) quite poor. Ramakrishna was a frail little man plagued by ill health. Anthony Sutich, who with Abraham Maslow pioneered transpersonal psychology, has been bedridden for years with arthritis. Aldous Huxley and James Joyce suffered from bad eyesight. I've even heard from a friend in the Rochester Zen Center of a woman in Japan, confined to bed, who began to practice Zen while flat on her back—and she came to enlightenment. (In Zen, enlightenment is verified by acknowledged masters who determine whether genuine satori has occurred to the meditator.)

I've made this extended analysis of Keith's statement because it is a key doctrine in TM and presumably represents Maharishi's own view. If I'm correct that it does, and if my examination of the statement is sound, then even though the words are Keith's, I've got to fault Maharishi for his mistranslation of Vedic thought into modern terms. Keith's statement shows a materialistic bias couched in scientific-sounding language, and its errors are compounded by a logical structure that is unclear and contradictory. On the basis of this statement, it certainly doesn't look as if Maharishi understands enlightenment—and if he doesn't, can he possibly be enlightened himself?

I *can* give Maharishi "enlightenment points" on another basis, however. A few years ago I was talking with a TM teacher about Kirlian photography. This is a technique by which objects are photographed electrically. The image you get on film usually shows a corona or halo of varying colors around the object, and many people at first thought this halo was the aura that some psychics clairvoyantly see around people.

The TM teacher told me that someone had once shown some Kirlian photographs of a leaf to Maharishi. In the photos the leaf was surrounded by a lovely yellow-white corona with energy streamers shooting out from it. The ribs and veins of the leaf were also glowing with light. Altogether it looked as if the leaf itself were really a by-product of an energy-field blueprint that shaped physical matter to itself, thereby producing or materializing a leaf. Maharishi reportedly looked at the photographs and then casually remarked, "Oh, yes, that's how things look when you're in God consciousness."

If Maharishi truly made this apocryphal remark, it indicates that he has developed himself psychically to an extraordinary degree, at least in a certain type of clairvoyance. Now, psychic abilities have always been associated with enlightened teachers of humanity, and in fact can be regarded as characteristic of those who are in higher consciousness. Maharishi himself consistently avoids any sort of psychic display, however, and won't even talk about such a phenomenon in public. All he says is, "Capture the fort and you'll own all the diamond mines," meaning, "Stay on the TM path rather than chasing up the dead end of psychic development and you'll have all the paranormal powers you want when you get to unity consciousness."

There *are* some people who have opened up psychically because of TM. A few have described their paranormal experiences to me, and they apparently include out-of-body projection and past life regression. But Maharishi always downplays this, and in doing so he is in strict keeping not only with his own yogic heritage but also with the heritages of *all* the world's major spiritual traditions. Psychic pursuits have always been identified as illusory byways off the path to enlightenment; seeking them in and of themselves is considered dangerous both to the seeker and possibly to others, for, if such a casual seeker attains psychic powers, he won't have the experience to use them wisely and morally.

The glamor of psychic powers is a trap, the enlightened say. Rather, seek God-knowledge, and in the process you'll naturally acquire psychic powers, along with the understanding necessary to use them properly—if you use them at all—for human benefit. Some people may need "signs and wonders" before they're motivated to seek higher consciousness, and for them Jesus and Sai Baba and others have performed supernatural feats such as materializations, healing the sick, and raising the dead. But these feats have always been performed as lessons or demonstrations to awaken people to their spiritual natures. In no sense was Jesus a miracle-monger, and in no way did he (or any other enlightened person) encourage people to attempt such feats themselves.

It looks to me as if Maharishi is "right on" with respect to psychic powers, and I give him a plus on the enlighten ment checklist. And, of course, if psychic ability were the only thing Maharishi had going for him, this book would never have been written. Quite obviously he has other traits that favorably impress people both within and outside the TM movement. He has incredible organizational ability and public relations skill—or at least an incredible ability to surround himself with people who can manage these things for him in superlative fashion. If there ever was a meeting of east and west, it's in TM, where the notion of spiritual seeking through the yogic life-style has been "cleaned up" and broken down into something akin to "How to Become Enlightened in Seven Easy Steps." For dispensing with traditional terminology (such as "chakras," "kundalini," "ananda") and traditional requirements (such as vegetarianism and breathing exercises) and then neatly packaging meditation so that it can be mass-marketed, Maharishi will surely some day be awarded an honorary degree in Marketing Science!

In Buddhist teachings it is held that insightful wisdom always needs to be accompanied by skillful means if there is to be any accomplishment. Maharishi has accomplished —in an extraordinary way. We must give him credit for this.

But Hitler also "accomplished" in his time. No one who has any sense of respect for human freedom and the value of the individual would credit a Hitler with noble motives and enlightened actions, and, thinking along roughly the same lines, many people have accused Maharishi of debasing the meditative life for commercial reasons. Others say that he is covertly working to establish spiritual fascism through thought control and the evocation of mystical overtones that will ultimately lead to psychic dictatorship.

I personally don't fear that Maharishi is trying to do such a thing. But I can see—on the basis of reports from several older men who have spent time in his company— why some people might think that he is. For one thing, I'm told that Maharishi still has enough ego left to enjoy playing the adulation game, that he really puffs up when he's surrounded by a group of admirers. Certainly he passes out blessings and bestows flowers on the crowd and encourages young people to assume the roles of disciples or devotees rather than of students. One of my informants said that he was quite turned off by "the fawning kids" and just as turned off by Maharishi's encouragement of the fawning.

This sort of game—gathering worshippers—is familiar enough to experienced observers of the spiritual scene; lots of "holy men" are playing it nowadays. Although yogic and other traditions see a guru-disciple relationship as being legitimate at certain stages of consciousness-raising, enlightened teachers of humanity have always stressed that the guru is only a means by which cosmic intelligence may begin to unfold the inner life of the disciple—a means to an end that is beyond both guru and disciple. Gurus' acceptance of people as disciples has traditionally been sparing and provisional; they have not been concerned with tallying a higher score on the discipleship scoreboard than their next-cave neighbors. A truly enlightened guru recognizes that acceptance of a disciple imposes a great responsibility upon him to bring that disciple as far as possible toward liberation—including liberation from a subtle but nevertheless powerful psychic dependence on the guru.

I hope Maharishi is concerned about this. But I must say that no one has battered down my door with tales giving evidence that he is.

On the other hand, the same man who mentioned "the fawning kids" does have the highest regard for Maharishi as an inspired teacher. When it comes to lecturing, demonstrating, and guiding people through meditational experiences, he says, Maharishi is no slouch. (This man, incidentally, is a college professor with many years of teaching experience and is himself favorably regarded by students as a genuine educator.)

Here's another thing to consider in asking ourselves whether or not Maharishi is enlightened. One traditional attribute of the enlightened person has been *vaikhuri,* the spontaneous flow of *jnana* or wisdom, both written and oral. In this regard too Maharishi must be given credit—his discourses in public and on television are usually quite articulate, especially considering that they are in English, which is not his native language. His speech and writing show a clear and simple style well suited to communicating with the masses.

Moreover, to the best of my knowledge, the content of what he says is usually doctrinally correct, the "real stuff" of Hindu and Vedantic philosophy. In other words, Maharishi seems to be straight here too, well in tune with the tradition he claims to represent.

Maharishi, whose name literally means "great seer," has published several books, including *The Science of Being and the Art of Living, Love and God,* and, more recently, a translation and commentary on the first six chapters of the *Bhagavad Gita.* According to a SIMS publication, a second commentary by Maharishi is forthcoming in which he will "connect the ancient descriptions of enlightenment with the results of scientific research on transcendental meditation in the fields of physiology, psychology, and sociology." Undoubtedly Maharishi has had editorial help with his writing, but that is understandable and acceptable, as long as the thoughts are truly his own.

Having commended Maharishi in these areas, I now have to point out that he *purposely avoids* making public pronouncements on controversial issues. Maharishi does not, for example, support pacifism like Gandhi, who practiced *ahimsa,* nonviolence, because he found it in accord with spiritual teachings. During the anti-war movement we didn't hear a word from Maharishi, so far as I'm aware, on the issues of militarism, nationalism, etc. In fact, Chapter 25 of *The Science of Being and the Art of Living* deals with the problem of world peace, and in it Maharishi specifically criticizes "many groups where people sit in silence and try to hear their inner voice, or the voice of God as they term it." Such practices, he says, make the mind dull. It is clear that one of the groups he refers to here is the Society of Friends—the Quakers—who are perhaps the best known pacifists in the world.

Maharishi has also recently let it be known that he believes in a strong military, and presumably he supports

India's development of nuclear arms—which significantly increases the world's chances of nuclear annihilation. If he does support this, it certainly isn't in keeping with goals two and five of TM's World Plan, which are to maximize governmental achievements and to use ecology wisely.

Nor does Maharishi have anything to say in public about other weighty philosophic issues such as sexual ethics, inequitable distribution of wealth, the possibility of life after death, or the doctrinal "errors" of religious paths other than his own (Hinduism). These omissions are too great for us to overlook. It may be that Maharishi is so totally focused on promoting a "simple, easy, and natural technique" of meditation that he decided early in his career not to turn anyone off by creating waves, but it may also be that he is simply ignorant of the issues or afraid of becoming involved in debate, and if this is the case—I'm not saying I'm sure it is, because I'm not—it certainly should lead us to wonder *why* he's ignorant or afraid, shouldn't it?

I've heard many stories about Maharishi, and some may have bearing on the question of whether or not he's enlightened. For example, I hear that every year he observes silence, fasting, and solitude for a week; each January 1 he enters a private room with only one glass of water and emerges seven days later after heavy meditation, with his batteries charged for the year.

I've also heard that Maharishi's nervous system is so "refined" that he not only can't eat meat, he also can't eat *any* cooked food that's more than a few hours old— the bacterial action would shock his system—so he has a private chef-disciple who travels with him to prepare his meals.

Some people have said that naming MIU after Maharishi was a colossal monument to his ego, and for them I offer *this* story. Michael Cain, who was present when the name was chosen, told me that Maharishi sought advice in the matter by asking simply, "How do they name universities in America?" When someone answered that they generally were named after people and often were named after major donors, he said, "Okay, we'll do it that way." Since everyone involved in the naming thought Maharishi had contributed most to the concept of the university, it was settled that his name would be used. No big deal about it and, as far as I can see, no big ego trip.

When we get down to the bottom line, though, *is* Maharishi enlightened? As I said, yes and no. He scores well in some areas, dubiously in others. And this armchair evaluation may be slanted because I've depended pretty much on what others who have first-hand knowledge (and whose opinions I respect) have told me. There is certainly room for rebuttal, and I'm open to correction.

I think the fairest thing to do is point to the ancient maxim about those who are spiritually seeking that says, "When the student is ready, the teacher will appear." And I would add that you get the teacher you deserve. Those who are on the spiritual path will not be denied by a God who works through the processes of a benevolent universe that gives us all we need every step of the way—including the apparently "negative" experiences. (The negative experiences, too, are learning situations in which cosmic intelligence speaks to us.) Those who wish to learn, spiritually speaking, will have their thirst quenched by a teacher in some form—a guru, a book, a learning experience, even self-searching. But there are teachers and there are teachers. The more you learn, the more you're ready to learn, and you've got to realize that if you're in, say, fifth grade, a college professor won't be the right teacher for you; if you're in spiritual kindergarten, you'll respond to someone who can teach and communicate on your level.

It's quite clear that Maharishi is communicating well at the spiritual kindergarten level. And doctrinally, he stands in line with some very great teachers of humanity. But whether he really has peer status with the spiritual equivalent of a college professor teaching graduate courses is another question, and I don't know the answer to it. I *can* say that I haven't heard of TM pulling many disciples away from other spiritual trips. And then, TM's dropout rate is rather heavy—about 25 per cent (although one study indicates that some return). I sometimes wonder whether those dropouts have gone on to first- or second-grade classes, or simply become disillusioned.

If Maharishi is sufficient for your needs, fine. If he's not, pack up and move on. Because if Maharishi is really enlightened, either he'll meet your needs as you progress through high school and college, or, happy in the knowledge that all paths lead to God, he'll give you his blessing as you walk away.

Chapter 12

THE FUTURE OF TM

Can science and commerce be blended successfully with the spiritual life in an organization dedicated to liberating the world from suffering and ignorance? Only if the answer to this question is "yes" does TM have a future.

Consider the scientific research. We've seen that some of it is being called into question, and even if most of it is eventually upheld, *all* the research reported thus far has involved subjects who are *not* in higher consciousness. Curing a million stress-induced migraine headaches tells us nothing at all about the neurophysiology of enlightenment—it only shows that TM can compete with other pop therapies.

If it is to survive, grow, and become recognized as a valid spiritual tradition, the TM movement must begin to state publicly and definitively what the characteristics of cosmic consciousness, god consciousness, and unity consciousness are. This it has never done. This is probably reasonable; since knowledge is structured in consciousness and can therefore be easily misunderstood or misinterpreted, it's not surprising that Maharishi might feel that such knowledge should be given only when the time is right—that is, when people are prepared not only to receive it but to understand it.

It would appear, however, that the right time has now

come. Maharishi has said that there are clear and definable criteria for determining who is in what state of consciousness; the SCI position is that if a person is in X state of consciousness, this can be empirically verified all the way. If this is indeed true, I feel that it should now be tested. And if the results of tests are as Maharishi predicts, fine—TM is validated; if not, we've still had a valuable lesson. (I understand from a TM teacher that the first steps in such a program have already been taken in the electroencephalography laboratory at Maharishi European Research University in Weggis, Switzerland. Observations thus far indicate that the problems associated with such research are great and that the neurophysiology of enlightenment is proving more complex than was anticipated.)

The future of TM will depend upon social research as well as laboratory research. One of the major sociological claims TM makes is that when 1 per cent of a city's population starts doing TM, the crime rate drops—or, as a SIMS publication put it: "One per cent of a city population practicing transcendental meditation has been shown by scientific research to directly improve the quality of city life of many cities in different countries." Dr. David Orme-Johnson, who is part of the research team reporting this conclusion, says that, with TM, the crime rate went down consistently in two hundred forty American cities while it increased in control cities in the same region with the same initial crime rates and with similar resident and college populations.

At first this reminded me of the old joke about the power of advertising that goes, "Did you know that since they started putting Smokey the Bear posters in subways, there hasn't been a single forest fire in New York City?" Dr. Orme-Johnson's own research shows that at least one control city (Fort Collins, Colorado) had a decrease in crime of 3.2 per cent, which is greater than the decrease for the least improved meditating city (Ames, Iowa), which achieved only a 2.5 per cent decrease.

Certainly we might ask whether drops in crime rate

are really *caused by* TM. Might TM be only grabbing the credit when the cause is something else? And, for that matter, is the decrease in crime rate real, or is it only apparent? The validity of crime statistics is almost as notorious as the criminals whom the statistics are supposed to reflect. Figures don't lie, of course, but you can lie with figures, and many politically sensitive police departments and city administrations have done so. Even the FBI has been known to juggle figures. "Crime waves" can be created with figures (and vice versa), just as you can create them by passing laws that make widespread practices illegal.

At the very least, the researchers have got to ensure that crime statistics used in the TM studies are being uniformly reported by all the cities, and that all are agreed on what they call "crime." If the alleged drop in crime among meditating cities means merely that fewer kids are turning on with grass and that therefore drug arrests are down but that rape, robbery, and murder rates are unchanged, a crime-drops-with-meditating claim for TM is, depending on your viewpoint, either a funny joke or a travesty of scientific research. (In fairness to the researchers, however, we shouldn't leap to conclusions. The researchers have yet to complete what Dr. Orme-Johnson says are "extensive studies on seventy variables on health, crime and economics.")

As it looks to its future the TM movement also needs to keep in mind the dangers of mixing spirituality and commerce. This was brought home to me powerfully as I was completing this book. I got a phone call from a friend, Mitchell Kapor, who is a TM teacher at SIMS Cambridge. Mitch is an intelligent, discriminating person with a warm heart and a tolerant attitude. I told him what I was writing, and he responded with some frank, well-intentioned questions. "If you criticize the TM movement for being commercial, John, how can you justify a title like *Everything You Want to Know About TM?* Aren't *you* just cashing in on a popular thing?" he asked me.

So, for those who might think me hypocritical, my

reply is as follows: I have no apology to make for this book. I earn my living as a writer and TM is a topic I have studied at length in the course of my research into and personal experience with the nature of consciousness and what I call "the enlightenment industry." This particular project is a sincere attempt to tell you everything you *ought* to know about the current phenomenon called TM—to give you a peek "inside TM" before you take the plunge yourself. Time will determine this book's true value.

On reflection, I must admit that this book is in roughly the same situation TM is, which means it's open to some of the same criticisms. "Publishing considerations" include a variety of elements: competing with other titles being pushed by *their* publishers; seeking and maintaining a positive cash flow; ensuring that the message is widely distributed and known. Altogether they add up to a marketing strategy for commercial competition that involves "pushing" a product. In publishing, that product presumably has social value.

Likewise, there has obviously been deep consideration of marketing strategy within the TM organization—and its marketing strategy has proven eminently successful. We may never know to what degree Maharishi himself is responsible for this, but whether he has personally been the guiding light or whether that credit belongs to his business advisors, TM—when measured by dollar volume—has "made the grade."

No spiritual path can be measured by its P.R. image and cash flow, of course. Yet if it is to operate within the world, some measure of worldliness must be allowed, and if it truly wishes to communicate with the masses, and the masses are in spiritual kindergarten, it has to gear its teaching and communications to that level. Even the most severe critic of TM must admit that Maharishi has packaged meditation nicely and has developed an extremely efficient organization for mass-marketing this simple technique. Still, it's difficult to accept the "sale" of spirituality or enlightenment. (To get some idea of the economics of TM, see Appendix II of this book.)

Any discussion of the future of TM must mention that Maharishi is getting on in years. He's now about sixty—no one knows his age for sure. When he goes *mahasamadhi*—this is the yogis' term for death, indicating conscious and voluntary departure of the spirit from the body—we'll be in a position to see whether the TM movement he established will endure and prosper in his absence.

TM may not be a religion in the strictest sense, but it certainly is a ceremonial cult with a theological belief system built around a single charismatic figure. Most such movements, history shows, have degenerated and died out after the central authority figure is no longer in control. Pop culture has given us many passing fads— the Guru Maharaj-ji trip, Ayn Rand, Silva Mind Control®, and so on. The new movements that have survived are those that reach us in the depths of our beings through seasoned wisdom and enduring truth.

Foremost among these, of course, are the world's great spiritual traditions. But even these have been rent and sundered. Christianity has known heretical sects and schisms. Buddhism has taken a number of forms. Orthodox Judaism has been divided by conservative and reform groups. Will TM also go through this?

My prediction is that it will. Even though Maharishi has taken measures to keep the movement intact after his death, change is inevitable, for change is inherent in life. "And this too shall pass" is one of the most profound sentences ever spoken. From my perspective, the question is really whether the coming change in TM will be a healthy modification and transformation to a higher level, or whether splinter groups will tear the movement apart through defection.

Maharishi hopes to avoid the latter by having extensive color videotapes made of himself. This way, the "purity" of his teaching will be preserved; the knowledge he revived won't be lost, thanks to technology, says SIMS, and humanity will not have to see the teaching degenerate as a new dark age sets in.

This is a plausible position, but my intuition is that

it won't be enough. Well, then, what if Maharishi hand-picks his successor, blesses him, and declares him heir-designate to the throne? This isn't likely, in my view, for the simple reason that there is no one in the TM movement with one-tenth the clout of Maharishi—there just isn't anyone visible who can be said to have unity consciousness *and* the personal magnetism, the show-manship, the marketing know-how, and the teaching ability of Maharishi—and this is the combination that made the TM movement.

Now let's consider that the movement is now spreading largely on the basis of word-of-mouth reports and the strength of scientific research that partly supports TM's claims. How long can this continue if more research is forthcoming to contradict the claims you read about today in the TM literature? And can you reasonably expect the same sort of worshipful dedication to an image on a TV monitor that Maharishi now enjoys in the flesh? No, of course not.

It seems likely that unless a worthy successor emerges while Maharishi is alive, a terrific power struggle will develop within the movement when Maharishi dies. Since nobody in the inner circle seems to have transcended his ego yet, personal differences and biases are likely to lead to diverging ideas and emphases among the people at the top. To the extent that these differences aren't settled, you have the makings of a revolution (or a "reform," as the losing breakaway group will undoubt-edly call it).

The issue that will touch this off? Money. With that in mind, I'll make another prediction. If and when factionalism becomes schism within the TM movement, it will be over the matter of "course fees." These fees are becoming exorbitant. Paying a hundred twenty-five dollars (the basic fee) for a total of six hours' instruc-tion is something a lot of people question. If TM is so great for the world, they say, why isn't it free—or at least a lot cheaper? This will become a greater issue as more and more TM teachers start building their bank-rolls.

In the early days of TM, few would have thought affluence possible for TM teachers, but now some of them are starting to pull in pretty good salaries. How long before they break out in new Cadillacs or racy sport cars? And what will *that* do for their image? What if it creates envy among other teachers?

As we've seen within the organized churches, there can be a caste system of sorts among the clergy—and brahmin status goes to the wealthy parishes the affluent members of which can afford to build and support a large, lavish church. TM has its equivalent centers in the big cities. If you're a teacher making a lot of money there, would you want to give it up for a poor and sparsely settled rural community where you'd have to work out of a spare room in your own home? Not likely.

Another thing the affluent image might do is create a breakaway teacher or two—there have been a few who have gone their own way in every movement from Protestantism and Silva Mind Control® to Ma Bell's monopoly on phone service—and these teachers might decide that they can go it alone, offering their services less expensively than when they were part of the TM movement. If you, the customer, can get the TM course cut-rate for, say, seventy-five dollars instead of a hundred twenty-five, won't you leap for it? Sure. And the teacher will be making out just about as well as he was before—or even better—because he'll be keeping 100 per cent of the fee instead of remitting it to national headquarters and then getting a fraction of it back.

One more way in which the movement might be split is by "revelation." It's happened many times before—someone claims to have a vision or a dream in which new knowledge—*correct* knowledge—is given from a higher source. Perhaps if this happens in the TM movement the person will even claim that Maharishi himself is the source of the revelation, having become the person's spirit guide from the other side in order to have him lead the movement into new paths. (This scenario could be quite interesting if several rebels claim to have a direct pipeline to Maharishi!) And so we can wonder who will become the Martin Luther of TM, the John Calvin, the Ellen G. White.

It seems to me that a breakaway movement is almost bound to occur for economic, philosophical, or psychological reasons. And when it does, the breakaway group will nevertheless want to maintain the TM mystique around itself. What will happen then? The new group will take a name very like the original; probably the name will be "transcendent meditation," or maybe "transcending meditation." How about "meditation for transcendence"? Or "Maharishi Meditation"? Or the "Movement for Maharishi's Meditation" (complete with its trademark, M³)? A splinter group might decide to emphasize the value of meditation for relieving psychosomatic problems, and call itself "medication meditation." Another group might address itself to a special group of businessmen under the name "mediation meditation." You can probably think up others just as silly.

Someone might accuse me at this point of indulging in making self-fulfilling prophecies, but I'd deny it. My influence within the movement is negligible, and in any case, Maharishi seems to be in excellent health and will probably be among us for many years to come. During the immediate future, he'll undoubtedly see the TM movement grow in strength. It may do this in part— ironically—because of the criticisms I'm making in this book, but I'd be pleased about that, for the true prophet —as opposed to just a negativistic critic—is one who gladly proves himself wrong. As my friend David Spangler of the Findhorn Community said in his book, *Revelation,* the true prophet is a false prophet because, by uttering prophetic words, he galvanizes people into positive action. The actions he thus sets in motion eventually offset or defuse the very events he prophesied, thereby proving him wrong—but this is what he wanted to happen in the first place. So, if this book causes the TM movement to "clean up its act" a little, I'll be glad to see my predictions proven wrong.

I'm not hopeful that I will be proven wrong, however.

Organizations and institutions have a way of becoming solidified and then entrenched; and when they've become entrenched, changing external conditions bring less and less internal response because those who've made it to the top are committed to an image of the organization that only "true believers" understand. Opinions become dogma, creeping bureaucracy sets in, the P.R. image commands more and more time and energy, and before the inner circle is aware of it, the world has passed them by. Their usefulness is outlived, and evolution has no further need of them. The spirit takes many forms, and when it's finished with a person, it departs. When this happens, as Timothy Leary wisely says, it's time to mutate.

As TM reaches its organizational peak over the next few years, we'll see whether it can avoid the mistakes of the past—avoid clinging to an empty shell after its purpose has been served.

Buddha himself foresaw the dangers of such a thing happening in his own "movement" and took steps to avoid it by emphasizing nonattachment to the teacher *and* the teaching. I suggest this as the key to TM's future. Without nonattachment, TM will harden into a self-serving institution that is only a sad caricature of what Maharishi presumably intends; with it, it will become an evolving program for service to humanity.

To close this book, I'd like to quote a friend. In *Transpersonal Psychologies,* edited by Charles Tart, Claire Myers Owens tells of Buddha's attitude toward meditation. "Buddha described his teachings as a raft to carry one across the river of life to the other shore— of enlightenment," she says. "Once arrived there, one is encouraged to discard the raft and even the Buddha, to stand alone, free and self-reliant." And I'd like to add that it's foolish to jump in the water and try to push the raft across the river. Furthermore, when your feet touch dry ground, there's no need to carry the raft on your back.

If the TM movement adopts this kind of perspective, and if Maharishi is revered as an enlightened teacher rather than slavishly adored as the savior of the human race, I think the movement can have a healthy future and an increasingly positive influence on the world. With a Buddhist outlook, the TM movement may even spawn rishis and maharishis who are beyond formalism and hero worship, whose lives are meditation in action, who embody the lines by Lalla, the fourteenth-century Kashmiri yogini:

> Worship was whatever work I did.
> Mantra was whatever word I said.

Chapter 13

AFTERWORD

After completing this book, a part of me wasn't satisfied that I'd answered in plain, simple terms the question of whether I recommend TM, So, briefly, here's my reply.

Yes, I would recommend to *most* people that they investigate TM, with the knowledge that it is highly simplified mantra yoga—beginner's meditation. "Investigate" means, naturally, taking the TM course and practicing TM faithfully according to instruction, as well as supplementing your experience with theoretical knowledge through reading, lectures, and, if possible, the SCI course. TM gets more sophisticated in later stages of the practice, and the guidance of a trained teacher is most valuable.

But "investigate" also means informing yourself about *other* points of view. Since some of the TM research is being questioned and contradicted, there may be a discrepancy of unknown proportions between what is claimed and what is actually delivered. If the claims are eventually disproven, it means that lot of TM meditators have been deluding themselves with grand notions of belonging to a save-the-world movement. (And don't forget that even if research eventually does substantiate TM's claims, it hasn't thus far dealt with the nature of higher consciousness—no experiments have been conducted using subjects who are clearly in higher consciousness as it is defined by TM.) You should also be aware that the claims for TM may apply equally to many other meditative traditions, some far more sophisticated than TM, but we can't say yet one way or the other, because no research has been done and official TM policy discourages such research.

As for Maharishi, I would caution you to view him not as a god but as a human being—or, more accurately, as a human becoming. If your TM experience proves beneficial, be grateful to Maharishi for what he has done, but don't expect miracles from him and don't slavishly worship him or his teaching (which is not consistent in all areas). To do so would be contrary to the development of self-actualization, which TM claims to deliver. Maharishi may indeed be very high, but he is regarded skeptically—for a number of reasons—by some whose opinions are worth considering.

Finally, you need to remember that history has proved all claims for instant enlightenment and quick, easy methods to higher consciousness to be simplistic, if not false. Not everyone needs a formal technique, but you certainly must be prepared to carry out the slow, difficult, and often painful "work on yourself" that alone brings intelligent character development, value-realization, and full integration into the human community. Without that effort, you're only fooling yourself into a bliss state that can be every bit as addicting as narcotics.

The practice of awareness never ceases. Enlightenment is an endless process.

APPENDIX I

What Is Transcendental Meditation?

by Harold H. Bloomfield, Michael Cain,
Dennis T. Jaffe, and Al Rubottom

Transcendental Meditation (TM) was introduced into
the United States by Maharishi (meaning "great seer")
Mahesh Yogi, who founded the International Meditation
Society, the Students' International Meditation Society,
and the Spiritual Regeneration Movement. Since his first
visit here in 1959, his technique has gained over 200,000
adherents. Its rapid spread can be traced to its ease and
immediate effects: it can be learned in a few hours and
is practiced for two fifteen- or twenty-minute periods a
day. Reportedly, beneficial mental and physical effects
are experienced after the first meditations. Hardly a
month goes by without a magazine article documenting
profound changes in businessmen, students, drug users,
teachers, families, and psychotherapists, who report increased well-being, relaxation, and energy, lessened
anxiety, greater perceptiveness, deeper relationships, and

From *What Is Meditation?*, ed. John White (New York:
Anchor Books, 1974). Copyright © 1974 by John White. Reprinted
by permission of Doubleday & Company, Inc. "What Is Transcendental Meditation?" was written especially for *What Is Meditation?*
and printed in that book by permission of the authors. It is based
on the book on the psychology of transcendental meditation called
TM* by Messrs. Bloomfield, Cain, and Jaffe (New York: Delacorte Press, 1975).

the alleviation of mental and physical symptoms of all kinds. They attribute these changes to Transcendental Meditation. Such reports have led to the scientific study of this technique, and the research reports have been so provocative that they have led many scientifically skeptical people to try it themselves. TM is a form of meditation that is particularly suited to active people who want to benefit from a practice without adopting a new religious doctrine or spending weeks or years at a monastic retreat.

TM is not a religion, a philosophy, or a way of life. It is a simple and effortless technique for expanding conscious awareness, which leads to improvements in many aspects of life. The term "transcendental" means "going beyond," and Maharishi claims that TM offers access to an unlimited reservoir of energy and "creative intelligence" that lies at the source of thought within the deepest layers of the psyche. Contacting this innermost source enables you to realize your unique human potential. This is done by letting your attention flow inward according to its own inclination, not by trying to force or direct it in any way. The experience of pure self-awareness has a profoundly revitalizing effect on all subsequent activity. TM, unlike other meditative practices surrounded by esoteric trappings and philosophies, requires no preparatory rituals, special setting, or unusual posture. It is not a special skill but simply the activation of a potentiality that every human nervous system is structured to enjoy. It can therefore be easily learned and practiced by anyone.

The practice of TM often leads to the experience of pure consciousness, a state of awareness in which you are perfectly alert while deeply relaxed, but not distracted by any specific sense impression, feeling, or thought. Meditators report this experience as "blank awareness," "being awake inside with nothing going on," or "not being asleep, but not being aware of anything in particular." Instead of the ordinary waking state of consciousness, in which you are constantly bombarded by a cascade of impressions, thoughts, and feelings, TM facilitates the experience of a state of restful alertness and pure awareness. This state is not a bizarre or unusual occurrence, for after their first meditation people often remark, "I've been there before" or "I felt that kind of peaceful relaxation when I was a child."

Maharishi suggests that pure awareness is familiar because it is the most fundamental aspect of the self, the source of knowledge and energy that has been described by exceptional people in all cultures throughout history. This fundamental experience of transcendence has been given many names, which together attest to its universality and supreme importance—*samadhi, satori,* Nirvana, the kingdom of heaven within, the Oversoul, the One, the Good, Being, superconsciousness, cosmic consciousness, peak experience, oceanic experience. Recently, Western psychologists such as Carl Jung and Abraham Maslow have begun to look more closely at the powerful curative effects of these experiences and to bring them within the realm of scientific study. TM allows a person to follow a systematic path toward this experience twice a day, making the possibility of self-discovery widely available.

TM consists of thinking a thought called a mantra (a Sanskrit word meaning "sound whose effects are known") over and over again without any effort to exclude other thoughts that intrude. When you learn the technique, a trained instructor selects a specific mantra according to an exact procedure. All mantras have a soothing and restful influence when repeated mentally. Their known effects are thus not due to their meaning, since they have none, but probably to their vibratory quality on the brain.

The sound of the mantra facilitates the inward flow of attention in a process often called mental diving. If during meditation the mantra leaves your awareness, you simply reintroduce it without making any effort to concentrate on it. TM is thus neither a strenuous process of concentration nor a deliberate effort to clear your mind. A meditator soon finds that the process of effortlessly thinking the mantra is not the contradiction it may appear to be. Since the ability to contact pure awareness is not a learned skill, but a naturally uncovered capacity innate in everyone, like speech or walking, it is not really an effort to allow the mind to move toward deeper levels. It is a spontaneously catalytic process which, once begun, becomes progressively deeper and more absorbing. Repeating the mantra allows attention to loosen its attachment to surface-level sense impressions and thoughts. Meditators often experience a state of contentment and relaxation in pure awareness—usually only for a few moments at first, but with greater duration and clarity as practice proceeds.

Meditators characteristically find the inward flow of their attention frequently being interrupted by the intrusion of thoughts, emotions, and sensations, a few of which may even be bizarre or dreamlike. Maharishi emphasizes that this process of stress release does not reflect unsuccessful meditation or something to be avoided. It is rather a recurring by-product of the meditative state—the release of stress from the nervous system. It has been suggested that the released thoughts and emotions constitute an analogue to dreams, which interrupt the nightly cycle of sleep but are necessary for the relief of psychic stress accumulated during the day. After a difficult day, you may experience considerable "unstressing" during meditation: deep and pleasurable periods of pure awareness, followed by the recurrent release of stress that has accumulated in the nervous system. There is no need to analyze or remember the content of thought that occurs in meditation. You simply return to the mantra when you notice you are not thinking it, without trying to push the thought out of your mind.

Many of the beneficial effects of TM on everyday life are derived from its ability to release accumulations of deep-rooted stress. The potential significance of a natural method of alleviating stress is underscored by the fact that a majority of Americans suffer from hypertension and other stress-related diseases ranging from heart disease and ulcers to anxiety neurosis, headaches, and other psychosomatic ailments. Maharishi defines stress as the physical imprinting in the nervous system of unduly excessive experiences that overload a person's faculties. TM counteracts stress by providing an equal and opposite state of deep rest. Maharishi accounts for this by what Elmer Green of the Menninger Clinic in Topeka calls the psychophysiological principle: For every event or change in consciousness there is a corresponding event or change in physiological functioning.

Every state of consciousness can be correlated with a characteristic physiological state. Just as bodily metabolism is affected by an anxious or angry state of mind, so the opposite is true—that relaxation beneficially affects the mental state. The physiological changes that occur in meditation can be measured to provide data on TM's effects, as we will report later. As a meditator experiences the mantra on subtler levels of thought, his metabolism changes in a measurable way—reduced mental activity allows reduced physical activity. Just as sleep and dreaming allow a complex psychophysiological regeneration to occur, so does TM activate a natural process for dissolving stress. We can conceive of stresses of all kinds as abnormalities that the nervous system tends to reject automatically, in keeping with the organism's innate urge toward health. All weakness is essentially due to lack of strength, and therefore cure or improvement depends upon directly strengthening the individual rather than just studying or coming to grips with the source of the problem. Knowledge of the source of stress may even be so unnecessary as to be demoralizing rather than therapeutic. A review of the current psychological techniques for relieving stress—including psychoanalysis, psychotherapy, group therapy, chemotherapy, and behavior modification—shows that they are either limited to a very few patients; take long years of personal attention from the therapist and lack reliable effectiveness; are specific to only a few kinds of stresses; may tend to restimulate stresses or stressful behavior without replacing them with strength; or merely make the patient manageable, without curing him. Empirical measurements comparing wakeful relaxation, sleep, and TM support the claim that the rest gained through meditation is the deepest possible, and therefore accounts for its powerful regenerative qualities.

By citing both modern Western scientific research and the ancient Vedic spiritual tradition of India, Maharishi explains why the technique of TM provides contact with the deepest center of the self and with what he calls creative intelligence, resulting in greater satisfaction, knowledge, and renewed ability to act creatively and in harmony with nature. The philosophical basis of his teachings are given at length in *The Science of Being and the Art of Living* (published by SRM Books and by Mentor as *Transcendental Meditation*) and in his new translation and commentary *On the Bhagavad Gita* (Penguin). It is too complex to be summarized here, but its essence is derived from the Vedas, which establish the source of all knowledge, not in external objects, but in the inner core of the individual, within pure consciousness. Modern Western culture has developed methods of technological control over the environment, at great sacrifice of knowledge about the self and the attainment of subjective values and truth. Only recently have Western psychologists, philosophers, and social visionaries begun to look for ways to redress the imbalance. They have begun to look at inner experience, at the internal basis of the self, at natural values and biological rhythms and laws, in an attempt to regain a proper balance of subjective and objective knowledge.

Maharishi's achievement has been to adapt the ancient technique and tradition to a modern Western format and to current scientific techniques of verification and communication. His personal background unites the ancient East with the modern West. He was educated at Allahabad University, graduating in 1942 with a degree in physics. Instead of pursuing a technical or business career, however, he became a disciple of his teacher Guru Dev, who transmitted to him both the technique and the philosophy.

Guru Dev taught those who came to him for guidance

a technique that originated in the Vedas, the oldest of Hindu (and possibly all human) oral teachings. The technique had been handed down from teacher to teacher within monasteries and in remote places. There had also been several periods when this teaching was made widely available to the public, such as the times of Buddha, Shankara, and Krishna. Guru Dev also made the technique available to all who came, not only to recluses but to those who were leading active lives and had families.

After Guru Dev's passing in 1953, Maharishi himself undertook a reclusive way of life, settling in a Himalayan cave from which he had no intention of emerging. However, as his meditation progressed, he felt some unfavorable influences and decided that his fulfilled consciousness must be responding to some quality in the atmosphere reflecting the sufferings of humanity. He left his retreat to attempt to relieve suffering by offering the technique to all who would receive it.

For months Maharishi traveled alone through India. Because of his monk's costume and appealing appearance, he was often asked to address a small gathering. When he did, he spoke about humanity realizing its full potential through a natural and effortless technique that allowed attention to be drawn within, not by religious conviction, but through a potentiality within everyone's nervous system. His message was enthusiastically received and thousands learned TM.

After about a year of traveling, he was given a ticket to fly to the West. Upon arriving in Hawaii in 1959, without a suitcase or any connections, he met people who set up a public forum for him. After instructing numerous people, he flew to California, where again helpful people set up a lecture program. These first sessions were so well received that a plan was worked out to teach the technique not just to people personally instructed by Maharishi, but in every community throughout the world. Maharishi would "multiply himself" by training teachers and creating a global organization to structure these activities.

Various nonprofit educational organizations were

formed, particularly the Students' International Meditation Society (SIMS), as part of the effort to spread effectively the practice of TM. Many people contributed time and money to these efforts, and the first teacher training course was held in Rishikesh, India, in 1961. A second course was held in 1965, and since then courses have been held three times a year in different places for increasingly larger groups. Now more than four thousand TM teachers around the world in various local centers offer introductory and advanced courses of instruction in the practice and its implications. The teaching program has recently been expanded to include a worldwide extension university, Maharishi International University (MIU), which offers videotaped courses, sponsors research on TM, and promotes symposia and academic inquiry into the Science of Creative Intelligence (SCI).

The spread of TM has been facilitated by modern technology. In addition to residential teacher training courses, Maharishi has made a color videotape cassette course in the Science of Creative Intelligence. The "World Plan" goal is to establish a meditation center for every million people in the world, including teacher training facilities. There are currently over two hundred centers in the United States. Formal academic courses on the Science of Creative Intelligence have been taught at over fifty universities, including Yale, Stanford, and UCLA. Maharishi International University has been formed in order to offer more integrated academic programs. The use of videotape hook-ups at TM centers will make MIU courses available to people all over the world.

Maharishi now acts as a teacher of teachers, and advises the organizations that teach the technique and disseminate information about the results and benefits of regular practice. The introductory courses have been structured to insure precise accuracy of teaching by means of systematic procedures for both teaching the technique and then verifying the correctness of an individual's practice. After learning TM, a person can come at any time for "checking": he meditates with a trained checker who can verify the correctness of his meditation and answer specific questions. There are also weekend residence courses where meditators practice the more intensive process of repeated meditations under careful supervision. This practice, called rounding, intensifies the process of contacting pure awareness and infusing creative intelligence. Meditators return from a weekend residence course feeling refreshed and energized. After about two years of regular practice, meditators are eligible for an advanced course of additional instruction and also may take training courses to become a checker or teacher.

The introductory course takes only a few hours on four consecutive days. All meditation centers offer two free introductory lectures describing the technique and its potentialities. Special lectures are also offered by request for an organization or professional meeting or even for a group of friends at someone's home. If you wish to learn TM after hearing the second lecture, you are interviewed by an instructor and agree to pay the fee ($75 for adults, $45 for college students, $35 for high school students), which covers not only personal instruction, but also four required follow-up sessions, regular checking, optional weekly meetings, and newsletters announcing special events and residence courses.

You then come by appointment for personal instruction. You are asked to bring a few flowers, a white handkerchief, and some fruit, to be used in a brief traditional ceremony performed in Sanskrit, in which the instructor expresses gratitude to the past teachers in the tradition. It is not a religious ceremony because you only witness it. It guarantees that you receive the technique as it has been passed down for centuries. Then you receive a personal mantra, selected by the teacher, and are guided into your first meditation with the teacher. The meditation is practiced at home twice the next day. All the students return the next evening for the first of three group sessions at which your experiences and reactions of the first day are discussed. At these sessions the whole process is more fully explained, so that you can relate what you hear to your own personal experience. Aftei this initial course, meditators are invited to make appoint- ments for personal checking as often as desired. A weekly check is recommended for the first month, and monthly checking thereafter.

While the effects of meditative states of conscious- ness have been valued since the dawn of humanity, it is only in the past decade that the scientific study of these states has yielded much data. Objective study of consciousness was made possible by the invention of such devices as the electroencephalograph, which mea- sures the electrical activity of the brain through the intact skull, and computers, which unscramble the var- ious brain waves into coherent patterns. Other physio- logical functions are correlated with different states of consciousness. Muscle tension, heart rate, blood pressure, rate of respiration, and the electrical resistance of the skin are measurable, and provide valuable insight into the connection between physiology and a person's subjective states of conscious awareness.

Nathaniel Kleitman and his associates in a sleep laboratory at the University of Chicago undertook the first studies that differentiated physiological correlates of the three common states of consciousness—sleeping, dreaming, and wakefulness. Studies of Zen monks, Indian yogis, and, recently, Transcendental Meditators in the United States have begun to provide evidence that suggests that meditative states of consciousness are quite different from the three ordinary states and have quite different physiological correlates and effects.

In addition to finding objective measures of various internal states, investigators of meditative states of con- sciousness have had difficulty in finding suitable sub- jects who were adept at their technique and in getting them to practice their meditations with monitoring de- vices like a mask over the mouth and nose to measure oxygen consumption, catheters in an artery in the arm to measure changes in blood chemistry, and electrodes connected to the skull and skin.

The recent spread of TM made it possible for large numbers of subjects to be studied in well-controlled laboratory settings. Because the practitioners were normal people, not religious ascetics, the results could not be attributed to factors like diet or the religious community. Also, the ease of TM meant that it could be practiced without disruption under laboratory conditions. For these reasons Dr. Robert Keith Wallace and Dr. Herbert Benson, of Harvard Medical School, chose TM for the most comprehensive study of the physiological correlates of a meditative technique. Thirty-six subjects of both sexes, some in Boston and some in Los Angeles, ages seventeen to forty-one and without physical or mental disabilities, participated in the initial study. They had practiced TM from one week to nine years, averaging two and a half years.

The procedure was simple. After half an hour for relaxing and getting used to the instruments, each subject sat quietly for about twenty minutes. This provided base-line measurements for each person, with which the changes during and after meditation could be compared. The subject was then instructed to meditate for the normal period of time, usually twenty minutes, and then to remain quietly seated for another half hour, to obtain a comparative set of post-meditation measurements. The three series of measurements were then compared.

Wallace and Benson's findings, reported in numerous articles, including the February 1972 issue of *Scientific American,* added considerably to the sketchy, often contradictory and erratic information from previous studies of yogis and Zen meditators. One of the most dramatic changes they recorded was a decrease in oxygen consumption. This is generally regarded as a measure of the level of physical activity, since it increases during exertion and decreases during rest. During deep sleep it drops to a point about 10 per cent below normal. Wallace and Benson found in all meditators an immediate, spontaneous reduction in oxygen consumption of 16–18 per cent. This began during the first minutes of meditation and was consistently sustained throughout. After meditation, oxygen consumption returned to normal, premeditation levels, indicating a return to a metabolic level ready for activity. To insure that their findings were not due to suggestibility or the mood of subjects in that setting, the changes were compared to changes reported for subjects under hypnosis. No decrease in oxygen consumption was found under hypnosis. Wallace confirmed that the decrease in oxygen was a natural phenomenon by checking that the decrease was accompanied by a decrease in carbon dioxide metabolism— another indication that the physical system is relaxed and functioning naturally, though at a slower rate, and not under any strain due to the decrease.

They also found a large increase in the galvanic skin response (GSR), which is the resistance of the surface of the skin to an electric current. This is widely used as a measure of decreased anxiety and is the basis of many tests, the most famous being the lie detector. If a person is relaxed and calm, not tense, the GSR increases. During deep sleep it increases by about 200 per cent. During TM, GSR increased by as much as 500 per cent in some subjects, indicating even greater relaxation and lessened anxiety. Dr. David Orme-Johnson reports in a 1973 issue of the *Journal of Psychosomatic Medicine* that Transcendental Meditators recover more quickly from stressful stimuli and have greater physiological stability than a similar group of nonmeditating students. Meditators recovered quickly when subjected to a sudden stimulus (a very loud noise), their GSR decreasing sharply for a few seconds and then quickly returning to normal. This autonomic stability has been correlated with measures of mental health. This state of calm alertness has measurable perceptual effects as well. Robert Shaw and David Kolb, of the University of Texas, found that TM practitioners had a faster reaction time than nonmeditators, and Graham, at the University of Sussex, England, found increased auditory acuity.

Another change reported by Wallace and Benson that strongly suggests decreased anxiety is the decrease in subjects' blood lactate, which was reduced by about 33 per cent compared to the drop in that of someone lying down or in the subjects' own premeditation relaxed state. The drop also occured at a much faster rate (300 per cent faster) than it does during sleep. F. N. Pitts reported in a 1969 article in *Scientific American* that people suffering from anxiety neurosis increase their blood lactate when subjected to stress, and even more strikingly, they become anxious when given injections of lactate. Furthermore, patients with high blood pressure often shown elevated blood lactate levels in a resting state. The low lactate level found in the TM subjects thus appears to correlate with their reported decreased anxiety and deep relaxation.

This biochemical change among meditators suggests a possible mechanism that accounts for their increased sense of well-being and decreased anxiety, and suggests that TM may be helpful for people suffering from hypertension. These findings led Wallace and Benson to conclude that the relaxation of TM was in some way a physiological counterpart to the "fight or flight" defense alarm reaction, which mobilizes the body to respond to threats and imminent danger or stress. Many people have suggested that our culture—with its tremendous psychological pressures, constant sensory overstimulation, and minimal physical activity—keeps us in an almost constant state of inner alarm, leading to stress and its related ailments. TM appears to slow down or counteract this alarm reaction and its physically and psychically destructive effects.

Another aspect of the Wallace-Benson research involved monitoring their subjects' brain waves. The characteristic change was an increase in slow alpha waves in the frontal and central regions of the brain, accompanied in some subjects by rhythmical theta trains, which are even slower waves, in the front of the brain. The frequencies and patterns are quite different from those seen in sleep and dreaming.

The TM brain wave pattern is consistent with Kasa-matsu and Hirai's findings with Zen monks who had been meditating for ten to twenty years and is thus a remarkable demonstration of the speed with which the TM technique produces similar results.* As in the Zen study, Wallace found that incoming stimuli were experienced by the brain clearly and freshly, but at the same time without interrupting the state of relaxation.

The meditative state is characterized by both heightened awareness and relaxation, so that one is not disturbed by every stimulus. Relaxation is associated with increased alpha waves. Studies of alpha conditioning, by which a subject learns to increase his alpha wave production, found that the alpha state corresponds with reports of pleasant, restful, tranquil emotional states. Research in progress at the Institute of Living, a private psychiatric hospital in Hartford, Connecticut, has looked in precise detail at the changes in brain waves in patients who have been taught either TM or alpha conditioning as an adjunct to psychotherapy. Preliminary findings suggest that TM is more relaxing and pleasurable for patients and may lead to more profound therapeutic results than alpha training. It also confirms and adds to the picture of brain waves during TM.

These and other studies demonstrate that TM has profound effects on the body. It sets in motion an integrated complex of physiological changes in the direction of relaxation, decreased anxiety, and a greater sense of well-being. These changes have led researchers to begin to define a physiologic state that is so different from the normal states—sleeping, dreaming, and waking —that Wallace has suggested it qualifies as a fourth major state of consciousness. He surveyed 394 regular meditators regarding their health; 84 per cent reported significant improvement in mental health, with most citing specific, concrete indications such as increased grades, lessened fears, and better personal relationships,

---

* However, similarity in physiological processes does not automatically grant spiritual growth and psychological maturity.— EDITOR.

and 67 per cent reported significant improvement in physical health, such as fewer colds, headaches, allergies, or even cessation of chronic ailments.

The effects on mental health suggest that TM can be conceived as a kind of self-administered psychotherapy. Therapy is available to relatively few people, is very costly, and does not produce consistent results for all patients. Therefore, meditation may be a very important additional tool for relieving psychological suffering. Daniel Goleman argues that meditation is a metatherapy that systematically decreases anxieties; he stresses the use of mechanisms that are familiar to therapists but that are more consistently and better applied through meditation. Meditation is suggested by more and more therapists, including two of the authors, to their patients. Preliminary reports suggest that meditation greatly enhances and speeds up the process of therapy, leads to deeper access into the psyche, and produces consistently better results than therapy without meditation. Its deep relaxation certainly contributes to its efficacy, but in addition we suggest that additional psychological effects of the experience of pure awareness favorably affect the patient's ability to deal with disturbing or unpleasant psychic material with a minimum of anxiety.

The most extensive research project using Transcendental Meditation as an adjunct to psychotherapy is being conducted at the Institute of Living and is headed by the director of research, Dr. Bernard C. Glueck. After nine months (as of this writing, June 1973) about sixty patients have learned TM; other groups have been taught alpha biofeedback conditioning and relaxation techniques to provide comparative data. Careful records are kept of their physiological changes; their progress in therapy; their behavior in the hospital community; their feelings about the treatment; their performance in school, if they are students (the institute has an accredited high school program); and what happens after they leave the hospital. Several teachers of TM are on the project staff, and members of the clinical staff have learned to meditate. From data gathered thus far, Dr. Glueck reports significant rates of improvement in the patients who practice TM, generally faster than previously. In addition, TM is well received by the patients, who feel that they are in control of the process and are responsible for the benefits they gain from the practice. This is in contrast to the psychoactive drugs, which, although recognized by the patient as helpful, do not give the same sense of "helping myself." Many have been able to reduce their need for medication, with marked improvement of sleep disorders.

The process of meditation apparently leads to an intimate and cumulative contact with the core of the self. This in turn promotes the process of self-discovery and growth. The resources of consciousness provided by the experience of pure awareness—the proposed fourth state of consciousness characterized by deep rest and mental alertness—seem to catalyze growth through the neurophysiological integration of the nervous system. Charles Tart, who has studied altered states of consciousness for several years and practiced TM for two years, reported in a 1971 article in the *Journal of Transpersonal Psychology* that the unstressing process seems to be a "psychic lubricant" that allows the release and settling of inappropriately processed experiences. In this sense TM may serve as a sort of "self-analysis" which proceeds naturally without any conscious direction or attempt to master one's past or present personality. Dr. Glueck notes that the thought content one may notice in meditation, though often of a primitive or even charged nature, is seldom if ever accompanied by the usual emotional charge or effect one feels in similar recollections drawn out during psychoanalysis or psychotherapy. He finds that some meditating patients can "work through" the significance of this material in relation to their illness in a much shorter period of time than is ordinarily the case—presumably because they are less bothered by recalling it in analysis or therapy after already having had it "played out" during meditation.

Many recent studies focus on the greater psychological health of persons who practice TM. Sanford Nidich,

William Seeman, and Thomas Banta in the May 1972 issue of *Journal of Counselling Psychology* compared the responses of fifteen undergraduate meditators with a control group. They used a well-known measure of self-actualization, the Personality Orientation Inventory, which measures characteristics of healthy, loving, creative, fully functioning people suggested by the work and writings of the late Abraham Maslow. They found that a meditator's sense of inner-directedness increases, as do the ability to express feelings in spontaneous action, the acceptance of aggression, and the capacity for intimate contact. Meditators seem to have better "psychic gyroscopes" and are more open to their own and to others' deep experiences and feelings.

Maynard Shelly, of the University of Kansas, reports on many years of studying the production and measurement of happiness in his book *Sources of Satisfaction.* His theory postulates that each individual has an optimum physiological level of arousal, below which lies boredom or unpleasantness. Some people prefer quiet, sustained pleasures, like reading or sitting with a loved one, whereas others enjoy highly exciting, risky, or stimulating pleasures, like mountain climbing. Every person has a unique ratio of both kinds of pleasure that makes him happy, and Shelly's work measures the degree to which a person reaches that optimum state. Shelly's students Landrith and Davies conducted several studies measuring the changes in happiness reported by samples of over one hundred Transcendental Meditators; the changes in these measures as their practice continued; and the responses of a control group of similar students who did not meditate. While people who started TM scored slightly lower than the control group in happiness, after a few months to a year of TM they seem happier and more relaxed; they experience a feeling of enjoyment more often; they seek arousal as much as nonmeditators (but avoid extreme excitements); they seek social contacts as often as nonmeditators despite the fact that they tend to spend more time alone; they develop deeper interpersonal relationships; and they depend less on their external environment to provide them with happiness, while relying more on themselves. Greater happiness, stability, self-sufficiency, and deeper contact with others seem to characterize meditators, and these measures increase as they meditate longer. Shelly suggests that meditators have more personal resources and energy to mobilize for their goals and are less affected by environmental setbacks. The results of all these studies suggest that TM is a unique psychophysiological process through which personal awareness of self, others, and the environment increases, along with the ability to achieve one's goals.

A great deal of the publicity about TM has come from studies, by Benson and Wallace among others, that report meditators decreasing drug use—not only illegal drugs but prescription drugs, alcohol, and cigarettes. Several studies, one involving almost two thousand meditators reported by Barbara Marzetta, Herbert Benson, and R. Keith Wallace in the September 1972 issue of *Medical Counterpoint,* show that over time, meditators lose interest in whatever drugs they had been taking. Of course, many young people turn from drugs to TM when they realize that the benefits they seek from drugs are not permanent, and they are therefore predisposed to cut down or stop drug use. Still, the response of adult drug users, who smoke, drink, and take tranquilizers or sleeping pills, tend in the same direction. Reports from therapists indicate that use of prescription drugs decreases as patients find TM lessening their anxiety and enabling them to sleep more easily. Similar evidence confirmed by newer studies has led drug abuse programs to investigate and offer TM as a way of helping drug-dependent people.

Several institutions—schools, prisons, and a business— have cooperated with researchers in conducting related studies that include the use of TM. These projects do not attempt to evaluate TM as a cure for illness but rather as a general method of helping people to improve their functioning and to enhance their well-being. In many instances, after an administrator or executive begins TM, he encourages others to try it and often asks a TM teacher to speak to his colleagues or employees. Numerous anecdotal accounts describe how one or more persons have introduced TM into an office, organization, or business, with positive effects for all who begin the practice.

Stephen B. Cox reported in the *Kentucky Law Review* on a study conducted at the La Tuna Federal Penitentiary in Texas. Twenty-three volunteer inmates/addicts were instructed in TM. Although results are not yet published in final form, preliminary reports are promising. David Ballou has reported informally on a project in the Stillwater State Prison in Minnesota, where fifty inmates were offered TM. Those who began TM were checked regularly and evaluated by a variety of measures. The results were positive in all the areas noted by other studies—decreased anxiety, reduced drug use, increased sense of well-being, and more positive motivation. Edward Morler is presently at work on a doctoral study of TM's effects in an organizational context. He is testing how the use of TM by employees in a bank will affect individual job performance. Several unofficial reports from public and private secondary schools suggest that meditating students improve their work, interact more easily with other students, their parents, and faculty, and voluntarily reduce their use of drugs. These accounts suggest that the personal benefits of TM carry over into a meditator's environment. One can only speculate about what might occur if school systems or corporations were to introduce TM. (In 1972 Haile Selassie, Emperor of Ethiopia, approved and began the introduction of TM into the entire public school system of Ethiopia.)

Evidence from psychotherapy, clinical neurology, child psychology, and studies of creativity support the basic tenet that the direction of human life is not arbitrary but is evolving along a definite path toward the actualization of maximum potential. The basic urge or drive in life is toward the full expression of one's talents and innate potentiality. The growing body of research evidence, supported by meditators' testimony, suggests that TM liberates previously untapped resources for the realization of these human potentialities. The truly miraculous capacities of the human brain and nervous system are still only partially understood at best and hence far from fully appreciated. Medical researchers are finding that fundamentally vital resources for improvements in health and well-being are found within the individual. Clearly the hope of our physical and psychical healers lies in effectively tapping these vital resources to achieve neurophysiological integration and the subsequent achievement of fuller mental potential.

This unlimited mental potential can be experienced as pure consciousness. When contacted regularly through the daily practice of TM, the value of this purely subjective awareness is infused into the mind and removes the limitations on the mind's full range of capabilities. The key to successful psychotherapy or to the most complete development of the normal individual is to create those physiological conditions that optimize the natural tendency of the nervous system to rejuvenate and reintegrate itself. TM can be learned easily and practiced naturally. It produces beneficial effects spontaneously exactly because it operates on the basis of this innate tendency. The ease and simplicity of the technique often seem startling to those who expect improved physical or mental health to be found through modern medical inventions or therapies, just because pathology and the allopathic alleviation of symptoms have been dwelt upon excessively in our society.

We can see that the optimal condition TM provides is simply a mode of functioning native to the human organism, maximizing deep rest and mental alertness. As the study of this proposed fourth state of consciousness proceeds, we expect to learn much more about the experience of pure awareness, its physiological correlates, and its effects. So far the consensus is favorable. As this knowledge spreads, the introduction of TM in schools, businesses, and communities will help to reduce the anxiety from which so many people suffer needlessly and to increase their growth and "self-actualization." Maharishi has said that man is born to enjoy and that suffering is alien to life. We find nearly all the prominent psychologists of the past several decades agree in their conclusion that man has an unchanging, intrinsically good inner nature that supports the growth of a healthy, happy, and fruitful life. The practice of TM will undoubtedly serve to make this inner strength available to more and more members of our society.

APPENDIX II

Fast-Growing TM Finds
U.S. Disciples Galore

from the *Washington Post* Service

Rose Reed, recently divorced and "doing some personal questing to get in touch with my spiritual nature," paid $125 one recent weekend for a 10-hour course in Transcendental Meditation.

She thus joined more than 600,000 Americans who have made Transcendental Meditation one of the largest and fastest-growing movements of the 1970s and a $20 million-a-year business in the United States alone.

TM, taught by an army of 6,000 in the U.S., is technically a nonprofit and therefore tax-exempt business that nonetheless holds large amounts of real estate throughout the country—and halfway around the globe.

The disciples of TM leader Maharishi Mahesh Yogi coolly offered $3 million for a 5,000-acre California site in the mountains overlooking the Pacific Ocean near the opulent castle built by William Randolph Hearst at San Simeon. They wanted the tract for their North American "Capital of the Dawn of the Age of Enlightenment."

It was the gesture of a movement that thinks big and has the assets to back it up.

The TM movement has grown from 25,000 persons practicing it in the U.S. a few years ago to more than 600,000 today, and an estimated 1 million worldwide. The organization lists 30,000 newcomers paying to join the movement each month—quadruple the rate of new meditators of just a year ago.

TM is sweeping across an America traumatized by a decade of turbulent protest, a disastrous war and the fall of a president.

TM blends an Eastern practice—the mental repetition of a meaningless word called a "mantra" during two 20-minute meditation periods each day—with such traditional Western values as the work ethic, clean living, personal achievement and conservative habits and appearance. Its enthusiasts say they suffer less anxiety and stress, are more productive and successful, and enjoy greater health and happiness.

Introduced into the United States in 1959 by a diminutive Indian monk named Maharishi Mahesh Yogi, TM flourished in the counterculture of California and attracted attention in the mid-1960s when such celebrities as the Beatles, Beach Boys and actress Mia Farrow went to India to learn the technique from Maharishi.

The movement's image has changed from that of counterculture fad to mainstream respectability. Professional athletes, housewives, businessmen and military men have joined the avid ranks of meditators, along with 10 senators and congressmen and more than 100 Capitol Hill staff workers. Some 30 public TM teaching and research programs involving alcoholics, drug addicts, prisoners, students and even civil servants have been funded by the federal, state and local governments.

A hardcover book describing TM and its effects—and advising readers to pay to join TM classes—has appeared on the best-seller lists. A separate softcover volume recently overtook "The Joy of Sex" as the nation's No. 1 paperback.

The TM organization comes complete with organizational trappings of corporate America: computerized mailings, high-speed communications links, even a well-turned medical and life insurance plan for its employees.

It operates almost entirely on the course fees it charges—up to $125 per person for the one-hour basic instruction in Transcendental Meditation, $20 to $30 a day for weekend retreats, $500 for month-long residence courses, $45 for the videotaped "Science of Creative Intelligence" course and up to $1,800 for three-month TM teaching training in Europe.

From its course offerings, the movement collected nearly $20 million last year and $40 million from 1970 through 1974, in the United States alone. All of it is tax-exempt. (The figures used in this article were obtained from publicly available tax records or from internal audits supplied by the movement itself.)

In the fiscal year ending Sept. 30, 1974, TM's World Plan Executive Council–U.S. received more than $14 million—including some $12.4 million in course fees, $250,000 in tax-deductible donations, nearly $1 million from the sale of educational materials and $62,000 from interest income. Maharishi International University, a four-year college at Fairfield, Iowa, centering around TM and the Science of Creative Intelligence, collected $4.4 million more.

Fees pay the U.S. movement's 6,000 teachers and feed and house many of the hundreds of low-paid, full-time TM workers. These persons are classified as "volunteers," according to movement lawyers, so that their room and board are not taxable.

The fees also pay mortgages and rent on TM-owned or leased properties across the country. And they are used to provide free European trips for TM teachers, about a $1 million subsidy in fiscal year 1974.

According to TM financial statements, the World Plan Executive Council–U.S. also contributed $1.9 million to support the Switzerland-based International Transcendental Meditation movement in 1974. WPEC–U.S. subsidized Maharishi International University in fiscal years 1973 and 1974, to the tune of $2.3 million in grants and interest-free loans.

Since most of the movement's revenues are spent as they come in, very little is invested, with the exception of some short-term certificates of deposit.

Course fees collected at every TM center in the United

States are sent to the movement's national headquarters in Los Angeles and from there are divided up this way:

Half goes to the local TM centers to pay expenses and teacher salaries, which are generally modest. Ten per cent is used for printing materials, 10 per cent for national administrative overhead, 15 per cent into an advance training fund for TM teachers' European trips, and 15 per cent for expansion.

"We need billions," says G. A. (Curly) Smith, a 53-year-old meditator and real estate developer from Boulder City, Nev., who has negotiated the purchase of many TM properties.

"We must make these facilities available to teach TM as quickly as possible," says Smith, a rangy Westerner who grew up in Oklahoma poverty. He became a salesman at 19 and now, among other things, is selling TM to whoever will listen. He is bullish on TM, but the movement's rapid growth is not without its problems, he says.

"It's like the tail wagging the dog," says Smith. "We're trying to keep up with the growth."

The TM movement's expanding—and heavily mortgaged—empire has come to include the following:

• Maharishi International University, formerly Parsons College, Fairfield, Iowa, being acquired for $2.5 million. MIU was established in 1972 and was located in Goleta, Calif., until its September, 1974, move to Iowa.

• Maharishi European Research University (MERU), established this year at Weggis, Switzerland, with an electroencephalographic laboratory to investigate "the neurophysiology of enlightenment." MERU's success, a movement press release says, "will be marked by lack of problems in all fields of life and in society as a whole."

• A commercial nonprofit "educational" television station, KSCI in Los Angeles, licensed by the Federal Communications Commission to begin leasing $950,000 worth of broadcasting equipment for KSCI. The top staff salary is $6,000, according to documents filed with the FCC. Much of the programming will be about TM and the theoretical Science of Creative Intelligence.

KSCI is the first of seven such stations planned for the United States by 1980. Other cities targeted by the movement for TM stations include Washington and Buffalo, N.Y.

• Undeveloped parcels of 160 acres in the mountains above Santa Barbara, Calif., and 57 acres in Rusk, Tex.

• A large publishing operation (MIU Press) with four presses and 55 employees, located at Livingston Manor, N.Y.

• Television production studios, audio equipment and a film laboratory, with equipment worth a total of some $2 million, also at Livingston Manor. "World Plan Television Productions," according to movement literature, ships over 1,000 hour-long video cassettes monthly to TM centers around the world, has produced over 200 tapes for Maharishi International University and duplicated about 10,000 copies of the 33-tape course in "The Science of Creative Intelligence."

• A fleet of 46 vehicles either owned outright by TM organizations or owned by others and used for TM business.

• Faded resorts turned into temples of meditation, called "forest academies," including Kickapoo Lodge at Lake Texarkana, Tex., which is leased; the 460-acre Waldemere Hotel complex at Livingston Manor, N.Y., acquired for $1.7 million; Hoberg's, a former big-band resort in the mountains northeast of San Francisco, bought for $358,000; a desert health spa east of Los Angeles at San Jacinto, once frequented by movie stars.

• In the acquisition stage is another retreat run by Catholic nuns in Indiana. Shelved, for the moment at least, is a plan to float a $7 million movement bond issue to pay for the purchase of many more "forest academies."

• Some 375 "city academies," centers for the teaching of TM. Centers in Berkeley, Calif., Burlington, Vt., Columbus, Ohio, New Orleans, La., and Cambridge and Worcester, Mass. are movement-owned. The rest are leased.

They are called "World Plan Centers" because the movement regards TM as more than a way to make individuals stress-free, more productive and happier. In January, 1972, the Maharishi declared that the widespread practice of TM could also achieve seven general goals for mankind.

Goals of the World Plan are to develop the full potential of individuals, improve governmental achievements, realize "the highest ideal" of education, eliminate age-old problems of crime "and all behavior that brings unhappiness to the family of man," maximize "intelligent use" of the environment, "bring fulfillment to the economic aspirations of individuals and society" and achieve the "spiritual goals of mankind in this generation."

It is a prescription, TM leaders say, that could fit almost any economic or political system, and that does not endorse or reject any.

The World Plan administrative headquarters are in Seelisburg, Switzerland, but resorts in Switzerland, France and Spain have been rented out of season to house Maharishi and his followers, who receive his personal instruction in teaching the ancient technique.

Maharishi (said to mean "great teacher" in Sanskrit) is said to be in his 60s, the product of an affluent Indian family of military caste and a formal university education in physics.

Maharishi says he learned TM from the late Guru Dev, to whom he has referred as "His Divinity," during several years spent in the Himalayas. To keep the teaching "pure," Maharishi and his movement maintain, only specially trained TM teachers can impart the technique and bestow the proper meaningless word, called a "mantra," on each meditator.

It is the mental repetition of the "mantra" during two 20-minute meditations daily that is supposed to produce positive effects.

The TM movement is "not at all democratic," according to its "national media representative," Peter Black. "Maharishi is very conservative. He believes in a strong military, a hierarchical structure."

Maharishi's retinue includes about 125 independently wealthy young adults, mostly Americans, who "hang around in a kind of studentship atmosphere," according to Black. They are also dispatched by Maharishi to fly around the world at their own expense spreading the word about TM and pursuing the goal of one World Plan Center for every million persons.

Maharishi has no legal, official or paid relationship with the American TM movement, which operates under the corporate umbrella of World Plan Executive Council–U.S.

But whenever there is a disagreement, according to Bart Walton, who worked for several months in the U.S. headquarters in Los Angeles, Maharishi is reached through the movement's telex network in Switzerland and asked to resolve the dispute.

"Everyone has such respect for Maharishi, for his basic integrity, you just want to trust his decisions," says Walton, 23, and now assistant director of the Hoberg's "forest academy" at Cobbs Mountain, Calif. "You know he's operating from a full mental level."

And Maharishi, according to Walton, played a major role in the acquisition of ailing Parsons College. "He just bargained them down" from $14 million to $2.5 million, Walton says, "like an Armenian rug dealer."

As the TM movement began to mushroom, Maharishi declared 1972 the Year of the World Plan, 1973 the Year of Action for the World Plan, 1974 the Year of Achievement for the World Plan and 1975 the Year of Fulfillment for the World Plan.

This unfolding timetable is based on the belief that one per cent of the population meditating will have a salutary impact on the rest, what his followers call "the Maharishi effect."

This effect was demonstrated, TM leaders say, by a survey of 240 American cities where at least one per cent are meditators: crime dropped an average of 17 per cent.

To sell TM, the Science of Creative Intelligence, and the World Plan, the movement combines Eastern tradition with Western technology. The marketing approach involves extensive use of color videotape cassettes, books and pamphlets, records such as "Something Good Is Happening" by "The Natural Tendency," posters and pictures of Maharishi and his late teacher, Guru Dev.

There is also a World Plan News Service based in Switzerland, with an admitted purpose of reporting "positive news" about TM, Maharishi and the movement.

The TM movement employs no outside public relations firm. It doesn't have to. Its built-in sales force includes teachers, full-time "volunteers" and state coordinators, who talk in terms of numerical "initiation" goals.

And the movement has another mechanism for expansion: teacher-training is a required course for all students at Maharishi International University.

Those in charge of the far-flung TM empire are mostly young, in their mid-20s to early 30s, and entrusted with responsibilities normally reserved for older people. Jerry Jarvis, a former reporter-researcher for the Congressional Quarterly in Washington and president of the World Plan Executive Council–U.S., is at 41 one of the oldest of the paid staff.

Many of the corporate trustees, however, are older men of means with established careers outside the movement in science, business or academia.

The TM organization began in the United States in 1959 with the founding of the Spiritual Regeneration Movement, a tax-exempt educational foundation that bought an airplane in 1968 for $55,000 and sold it two years later at a $26,000 loss, according to federal tax returns.

The Spiritual Regeneration Movement, now seeking to enlist older people into the ranks of meditators, survives with a small budget as one of. several groups consolidated in 1974 under the World Plan Executive Council.

The other branches of the movement are Students' International Meditation Society, International Meditation Society for the general populace, and the American Foundation for the Science of Creative Intelligence for business and management.

APPENDIX III

A Historical Note on Mantra Meditation

by Herbert Benson

The elicitation of the relaxation response has been a part of many secular and religious practices for centuries.

In the West, a fourteenth century Christian treatise entitled *The Cloud of Unknowing* discusses how to attain an alleged union with God. The anonymous author states that this goal cannot be reached in the ordinary levels of human consciousness but requires the use of "lower" levels. These levels are reached by eliminating all distractions and physical activity, all worldly things, including all thoughts. As a means of "beating down thought," the use of a single-syllable word, such as "God" or "love," should be repeated:

> Choose whichever one you prefer, or, if you like, choose another that suits your taste, provided that it is of one syllable. And clasp this word tightly in your heart so that it never leaves it no matter what may happen. This word shall be your shield and your spear. . . . With this word you shall strike down thoughts of every kind and drive them beneath

From "Your Innate Asset for Combating Stress," originally published in the *Harvard Business Review,* July/August 1974. "A Historical Note on Mantra Meditation" is reprinted by permission of the *Harvard Business Review.*

the cloud of forgetting. After that, if any thoughts
should press upon you . . . answer them with this
word only and with no other words.

According to the writer, there will be moments when
"every created thing may suddenly and completely be
forgotten. But immediately after each stirring, because
of the corruption of the flesh, [the soul] drops down
again to some thought or some deed." An important
instruction for success is "do not by another means
work in it with your mind or with your imagination."

Another Christian work, *The Third Spiritual Alphabet,* written in the tenth century by Fray Francisco de
Osuna, describes an altered state of consciousness. He
wrote that "contemplation requires us to blind ourselves
to all that is not God," and that one should be deaf
and dumb to all else and must "quit all obstacles, keeping your eyes bent on the ground." The method can be
either a short, self-composed prayer, repeated over and
over, or simply saying *no* to thoughts when they occur.
This exercise was to be performed for one hour in the
morning and evening and taught by a qualified teacher.

Fray Francisco wrote that such an exercise would
help in all endeavors, making individuals more efficient
in their tasks and the tasks more enjoyable; that all men,
especially the busy, secular as well as religious, should
be taught this meditation because it is a refuge to which
one can retreat when faced with stressful situations.

Christian meditation and mysticism were well developed within the Byzantine church and known as
Hesychasm. Hesychasm involved a method of repetitive
prayer which was described in the fourteenth century
at Mount Athos in Greece by Gregory of Sinai and was
called "The Prayer of the Heart" or "The Prayer of
Jesus." It dates back to the beginnings of Christianity.
The prayer itself was called secret meditation and was
transmitted from older to younger monks through an
initiation rite. Emphasis was placed on having a skilled
instructor. The method of prayer recommended by these
monks was as follows:

Sit down alone and in silence. Lower your head, shut your eyes, breathe out gently, and imagine yourself looking into your own heart. Carry your mind, i.e., your thoughts, from your head to your heart. As you breathe out, say "Lord Jesus Christ, have mercy on me." Say it moving your lips gently, or simply say it in your mind. Try to put all other thoughts aside. Be calm, be patient, and repeat the process very frequently.

In Judaism, similar practices date back to the time of the second temple in the second century B.C. and are found in one of the earliest forms of Jewish mysticism, Merkabalism. In this practice of meditation, the subject sat with his head between his knees and whispered hymns, songs, and repeated a name of a magic seal.

In the thirteenth century A.D., the works of Rabbi Abulafia were published, and his ideas became a major part of Jewish Kabbalistic tradition. Rabbi Abulafia felt that the normal life of the soul is kept within limits by our sensory perceptions and emotions, and since these perceptions and emotions are concerned with the finite, the soul's life is finite. Man, therefore, needs a higher form of perception which, instead of blocking the soul's deeper regions, opens them up. An "absolute" object on which to meditate is required. Rabbi Abulafia found this object in the Hebrew alphabet. He developed a mystical system of contemplating the letters of God's name. Rabbi Ben Zion Bokser describes Rabbi Abulafia's prayer:

Immersed in prayer and meditation, uttering the divine name with special modulations of the voice and with special gestures, he induced in himself a state of ecstasy in which he believed the soul had shed its material bonds and, unimpeded, returned to its divine source.*

---

* From the *World of the Cabbalah* (New York: Philosophical Library, 1954), p. 9.

The purpose of this prayer and methodical meditation is to experience a new state of consciousness in which all relation to the senses is severed. Gershom Gerhard Scholem compares this state to music and yoga. He feels that Abulafia's teachings "represent but a Judaized version of that ancient spiritual technique which has found its classical expression in the practices of the Indian mystics who follow the system known as *Yoga*." Scholem continues:

To cite only one instance out of many, an important part in Abulafia's system is played by the technique of breathing; now this technique has found its highest development in the Indian *Yoga*, where it is commonly regarded as the most important instrument of mental discipline. Again, Abulafia lays down certain rules of body posture, certain corresponding combinations of consonants and vowels, and certain forms of recitation, and in particular some passages of his book *The Light of the Intellect* give the impression of a Judaized treatise on *Yoga*. The similarity even extends to some aspects of the doctrine of ecstatic vision, as preceded and brought about by these practices.*

The basic elements that elicit the relaxation response in certain practices of Christianity and Judaism are also found in Islamic mysticism or Sufism. Sufism developed in reaction to the external rationalization of Islam and made use of intuitive and emotional faculties which are claimed to be dormant until utilized through training under the guidance of a teacher. The method of employing these faculties is known as Dhikr. It is a means of excluding distractions and of drawing nearer to God by the constant repetition of His name, either silently or aloud, and by rhythmic breathing. Music, musical poems, and dance are also employed in their ritual of Dhikr, for

---

* *Major Trends in Jewish Mysticism* (New York: Schocken Books, 1967), p. 139.

it was noticed that they could help induce states of ecstasy.

Originally, Dhikr was only practiced by the members of the society who made a deliberate choice to redirect their lives to God as the preliminary step in the surrender of the will. Upon initiation into his order, the initiate received the *wird,* a secret, holy sound. The old Masters felt that the true encounter with God could not be attained by all, for most men are born deaf to mystical sensitivity. However, by the twelfth century, this attitude had changed. It was realized that this ecstasy could be induced in the ordinary man in a relatively short time by rhythmic exercises involving posture, control of breath, coordinated movements, and oral repetitions.

In the Western world, the relaxation response elicited by religious practices was not part of the routine practice of religions, but rather was associated with the mystical tradition. In the East, however, meditation that elicited the relaxation response was developed much earlier and became a major element in religion as well as in everyday life. Writings from Indian scriptures, the Upanishads, dated sixth century B.C., note that individuals might attain "a unified state with the Brahman [the Deity] by means of restraint of breath, withdrawal of senses, meditation, concentration, contemplation, and absorption."

There are a multitude of Eastern religions and ways of life, including Zen and Yoga with their many variants, which can elicit the relaxation response. They employ mental and physical methods, including the repetition of a word or sound, the exclusion of meaningful thoughts, a quiet environment, a comfortable position, and they stress the importance of a trained teacher. One of the meditative practices of Zen Buddhism, Zazen, employs a yoga-like technique for the coupling of respiration and counting to ten, e.g., one on inhaling, two on exhaling, and so on, to ten. With time, one stops counting and simply "follows the breath" in order to achieve a state of no thought, no feeling, to be completely in nothing.

Shintoism and Taoism are important religions of Japan

and China. A method of prayer in Shintoism consists of sitting quietly, inspiring through the nose, holding inspiration for a short time, and expiring through the mouth, with eyes directed toward a mirror at their level. Throughout the exercise, the priest repeats ten numbers, or sacred words, pronounced according to the traditional religious teachings. Fujisawa noted, "It is interesting that this grand ritual characteristic of Shintoism is doubtlessly the same process as *Yoga.*" Taoism, one of the traditional religions of China, employs, in addition to methods similar to Shinto, concentration on nothingness to achieve absolute tranquility.

Similar meditational practices are found in practically every culture of man. Shamanism is a form of mysticism associated with feelings of ecstasy and is practiced in conjunction with tribal religions in North and South America, Indonesia, Oceania, Africa, Siberia, and Japan. Each shaman has a song or chant to bring on trances, usually entering into solitude to do so. Music, especially the drum, plays an important part in Shamanistic trances.

Many less traditional religious practices are flourishing in the United States. One aim of the practices is achievement of an altered state of consciousness, which is induced by techniques similar to those that elicit the relaxation response. Subud, Nichiren Sho Shu, Hare Krishna, Scientology, Black Muslimism, the Meher Baba group, and the Association for Research and Enlightenment are but a few of these.

In addition to techniques that elicit the relaxation response within a religious context, secular techniques also exist. The so-called nature mystics have been able to elicit the relaxation response by immersing themselves in quiet, often in the quiet of nature. Wordsworth believed that when his mind was freed from preoccupation with disturbing objects, petty cares, "little enmities and low desires," he could reach a condition of equilibrium which he described as a "wise passiveness" or "a happy stillness of the mind." Wordsworth believed that anyone could deliberately induce this condition in himself by a kind of relaxation of the will. Thoreau made many references to such feelings attained by sitting for hours alone with nature. Indeed, Thoreau compares himself to a yogi. William James describes similar experiences. For the reader who wishes to pursue the topic further, a treatise on other such experiences may be found in Raynor C. Johnson's *Watcher on the Hills* (Mystic, Connecticut; Lawrence Verry, Inc., 1951).

GLOSSARY OF TM TERMS

The following terms are frequently met in promotional literature about transcendental meditation, but, with the exception of "mantra," "Science of Creative Intelligence," and "transcendental meditation," they are not defined in any public documents—at least not in any that I could find, and I checked with several SIMS centers and asked personnel there for glossaries. So, pending official pronouncements, I offer my personal attempt to create a glossary of TM terms.

—JOHN WHITE

Academy for the Science of Creative Intelligence (ASCI). A facility for weekend residence courses (see below), advanced meditation training, the basic Science of Creative Intelligence course (see below) and Phase I teacher training. Academies are located at Livington Manor, New York, and in several places in California.

American Foundation for the Science of Creative Intelligence (AFSCI). The American branch of the International Foundation for the Science of Creative Intelligence (see below).

Checker. A person trained to verify correct meditation through a set, systematic procedure involving questions to be asked of the meditator.

Checking. A set, systematic procedure for verifying correct meditation. Questions asked by a checker and answered by the meditator are designed to indicate where re-instruction is needed.

Forest academy. A one-month program of intensive meditation and study scheduled approximately every three months in the regular undergraduate program at Maharishi International University (see below).

Initiator. A teacher of transcendental meditation trained by Maharishi Mahesh Yogi.

Initiation. The ceremony through which a person is formally admitted to the practice of transcendental meditation under the instruction of an initiator.

International Foundation for the Science of Creative Intelligence (IFSCI). The organization within the transcendental meditation movement given primary responsibility for delivering the TM message to the business and industrial community.

International Meditation Society (IMS). The organization within the transcendental meditation movement given primary responsibility for delivering the TM message to the general public.

Maharishi International University (MIU). A four-year, degree-granting educational institution with its main campus in Fairfield, Iowa; its purpose is to help implement the World Plan (see below) by unfolding the full potential of the individual on the basis of the Science of Creative Intelligence (see below) through academic study, field work, and forest academy (see above) programs. External degree and non-degree programs are available or soon will be.

Mantra. A sound the effects of which are known, used during transcendental meditation as the focus of attention. It is silently repeated over and over by the meditator.

Residence course. A weekend, open to all transcendental meditators, of intensive meditation and further instruction in TM.

Science of Creative Intelligence (SCI). The knowledge of the nature, origin, range, growth, and application of creative intelligence. This science arose from the major discovery that there exists in every human being a constant source of intelligence, energy, and happiness. *Science*—a systematic investigation by means of repeatable experiment to gain useful and testable knowledge. *Creative*—having and displaying creativity, the cause of change everywhere at all times, generating new expressions of life, progressive and evolutionary in nature. *Creative intelligence*—the single and branching flow of energy (creativity) and directedness (intelligence).

Spiritual Regeneration Movement (SRM). The organization within the transcendental meditation movement given primary responsibility for delivering the TM message to spiritual or religious-minded people.

Stress. Hypothetical blockages in the human nervous system that keep it from operating maximally, thereby limiting the quality and scope of mental life.

Students' International Meditation Society (SIMS). The organization within the transcendental meditation movement given primary responsibility for delivering the TM message to students and the academic community.

Transcendental meditation (TM). The practical aspect of the Science of Creative Intelligence (see above); a simple, natural, and effortless mental technique practiced twenty minutes twice a day. During meditation, the individual experiences progressively quieter levels of thought until he transcends thought and experiences its source—the field of pure creative intelligence, that silent, unbounded state of awareness that gives rise to all impulses of thought, feeling, and action. *Transcendental*—going beyond.

Vedas. The earliest Hindu sacred writings. Adjective—Vedic.

World Plan. A plan, adopted in 1972, to progressively unfold the full potential of every individual through the principles and practice of the Science of Creative Intelligence (see above). It is intended that, ultimately, one teacher of transcendental meditation will be available for every one thousand persons in the world, and through them the World Plan will: (1) develop the full potential of the individual, (2) improve governmental achievements, (3) realize the highest ideal of education, (4) eliminate the age-old problem of crime and all behavior that brings unhappiness to humanity, (5) maximize the intelligent use of the environment, (6) bring fulfillment to the economic aspirations of individuals and society, and (7) achieve the spiritual goals of humanity within one generation. (The goal of a World Plan center for every one million people in the world has already been achieved.)

World Plan Administrative Center. World Plan headquarters in Seelisberg, Switzerland.

World Plan Executive Council (WPEC). The coordinating body for all the various branches and organs of the transcendental meditation movement throughout the world, consisting of the presidents of the Spiritual Regeneration Movement, International Meditation Society, Students' International Meditation Society, Maharishi International University, and the International Foundation for the Science of Creative Intelligence, and a board of advisors and a board of directors.

SUGGESTED READINGS

Bloomfield, Harold, Cain, Michael, and Jaffe, Dennis. *TM*: Discovering Inner Energy and Overcoming Stress.* New York: Delacorte Press, 1975.

Bucke, R. M. *Cosmic Consciousness.* New York: E. P. Dutton & Co., 1970.

Campbell, Anthony. *Seven States of Consciousness.* New York: Perennial Library, 1974.

Denniston, Denise, and McWilliams, Peter. *The TM Book.* Los Angeles: Versemonger Press, 1975.

Forem, Jack. *Transcendental Meditation.* New York: E. P. Dutton & Co., 1974.

Hansen, Virginia. *Approaches to Meditation.* Wheaton, Ill.: Quest Books, 1973.

Huxley, Aldous. *The Perennial Philosophy.* New York: Harper & Row, Publishers, 1945.

Kanellakos, Demetri, and Lukas, Jerome. *The Psychology of Transcendental Meditation.* Menlo Park, Calif.: W. A. Benjamin, 1974.

Kapleau, Philip. *The Three Pillars of Zen.* Boston: Beacon Press, 1965.

Krishna, Gopi. *Kundalini.* Berkeley, Calif.: Shambhala Publications, 1971.

———. *The Secret of Yoga.* New York: Harper & Row, Publishers, 1972.

————. *Higher Consciousness*. New York: Julian Press, 1974.

————. *The Awakening of Kundalini*. New York: E. P. Dutton & Co., 1975.

LeShan, Lawrence. *How to Meditate*. New York: Bantam Books, 1975.

Maslow, Abraham. *Toward a Psychology of Being*. New York: D. Van Nostrand Co., 1968.

Musès, Charles, and Young, Arthur. *Consciousness and Reality*. New York: Avon Books, 1974.

Ornstein, Robert. *The Nature of Human Consciousness*. New York: The Viking Press, 1973.

————. *The Psychology of Consciousness*. San Francisco: W. H. Freeman and Co., Publishers, 1972.

Robbins, Jhan, and Fisher, David. *Tranquility Without Pills*. New York: Peter H. Wyden, 1972.

Rosenfeld, Edward. *The Book of Highs*. New York: Quadrangle Books, 1973.

Tart, Charles. *Altered States of Consciousness*. New York: Anchor Books, 1972.

Weil, Andrew. *The Natural Mind*. Boston: Houghton Mifflin Co., 1972.

White, John. *Frontiers of Consciousness*. New York: Julian Press, 1974; and New York: Avon Books, 1975.

————. *The Highest State of Consciousness*. New York: Anchor Books, 1972.

————. *What Is Meditation?* New York: Anchor Books, 1974.

Yogi, Maharishi Mahesh. *Transcendental Meditation*. New York: Signet Books, 1973. Originally published in 1966 as *The Science of Being and the Art of Living*.

P A R A ▼ I E W

PARAVIEW publishes quality works
that focus on body, mind, and spirit;
the frontiers of science and culture;
and responsible business—
areas related to the transformation of society.

PARAVIEW PUBLISHING offers books via three imprints.
PARAVIEW POCKET BOOKS are traditionally published books
co-published by Paraview and Simon & Schuster's Pocket Books.
PARAVIEW PRESS and *PARAVIEW SPECIAL EDITIONS*
use digital print-on-demand technology to create
original paperbacks for niche audiences,
as well as reprints of previously out-of-print titles.

For a complete list of **PARAVIEW** Publishing's books
and ordering information, please visit our website at
www.paraview.com, where you can also sign up
for our free monthly media guide.

TRANSFORMING THE WORLD
ONE BOOK AT A TIME

Lightning Source UK Ltd.
Milton Keynes UK
11 August 2010
158212UK00001B/20/A